Backstage Passes

Rock 'n' Roll Life in the Sixties

by Al Kooper

with Ben Edmonds

STEIN AND DAY/*Publishers*/New York

ML
420   2
.K8
A3

First published in 1977
Copyright © 1977 by Al Kooper
All rights reserved
Designed by Ed Kaplin
Printed in the United States of America
Stein and Day/*Publishers*/Scarborough House,
Briarcliff Manor, N.Y. 10510

Library of Congress Cataloging in Publication Data

Kooper, Al.
   Backstage passes

    1. Kooper, Al.   2. Rock musicians—Correspondence, reminiscences, etc.   I. Edmonds, Ben, joint author. II. Title.
ML420.K8A3   784'.092'4 [B]   75-11758
ISBN 0-8128-1840-7   Paperback ISBN 0-8128-2171-1

This book is dedicated:

To Brian Wilson for opening untold doors and naming my son
To my son Brian for opening anything he can get his hands on
To Bob Dylan for coming to see me play in Minnesota in the late fifties
To my folks for being much more realistic than "All in the Family"
To Mick Jagger for sending me the tape to "You Can't Always Get What You Want" and letting me do whatever I wanted to it
To Muddy Waters for being real
To Maynard Ferguson for Blood Sweat and Tears
To my first wife for parting with some great photos for this edition
To my second wife for somehow surviving it all
To Jimi Hendrix for inventing my favorite dinner and for the black Strat I still play today
To David Clayton-Thomas for giving me a rest
To Sid Bernstein for a great pair of hands
To my sister Patti for staying out of the country
To Paul Simon for the club gigs and *Music of Bulgaria*
To Ringo for moving into my house
To David Cassidy for moving out of it
To Andy Kulberg for being so fucking funny
To Elton John and Chicago for remembering
To Larry Carlton for a great solo album
To Jim Gribble, Leo Rogers, Aaron Schroeder and the Blues Project for picking me up off the streets
To Blood Sweat and Tears for putting me back on them
To Clive Davis for putting his book out first
To Tom Wilson for graduating from Harvard
To Danny Kalb for teaching me the blues
To Steve Katz for giving me the blues
To Roy Blumenfeld for living them
To John Simon for teaching me more than he'll ever know

To Garry Nichamin for being funny and feeding me old records
To Tony Loew for introducing me to everyone
To Sharon Lawrence for introducing me to Tony Loew
To Stan Polley for putting up with everything with a straight face
To three eggs over medium, a toasted buttered English, and a large grade A, which have sustained me most of my adult life without any fear of cholesterol
To Big Debbie & Little Debbie for knowing when to come and go
To Mickey Finn for scaring the shit out of anyone who rang the doorbell or the telephone
To Freddie Lipsius for being the best
To Henry & Manny's Music Store for nineteen years of at *least* 40 percent off
To all my relatives for understanding why I don't appear at weddings, funerals, bar mitzvahs, divorce parties and other gatherings of the tribe
To Sol Stein for his patience
To Drs. Canter, Lavett, Loel, Morgan, and Kerner for keeping the machine functioning
To Maria, Jayne, Mimi, Patti, and Debbie for pretending to be secretaries
To Ben at PIPs for always having a table
To Domenic Frontiere for hangin' 'em high
To The University Inn in Coral Gables, Florida, for the best key lime pie in the world
To Eric Krackow for being half of me while I grew up
To Howard Farber who, when asked what he did for a living by a fellow member of the PTA, replied: Oh I make fuck films
To Phil Dossick for corruption mental, physical, and musical
To Birtha for showin' it could be done
To Mose Jones (R.I.P.) for being misunderstood and real good
To Dianne for taking my virginity
To Joanie for giving it back
To Gately and Childstar for countless hours of amusement and for heading up my NY ratpack

To Lou Christie for getting a hit record every two years so's I can set my watch

To Julio for being the queen bee of the Hollyweird divorcees and suing Gregg Allman *before* Cher (five points)

To Arthur Eaton for making out OK

To Gallini, Magoody, Chevvie, and Fiat, my dear departed doggies

To Ken Kendall, Wartoke, Gibson, Stromberg, Sharon, and Norman for making people believe otherwise

To Bobby Colomby for laughing so hard

To his brother Jules for describing me as an "electrified King Hussein"

To Ray Charles for everything including the hair under his bottom lip

To Horace Silver and Bobby Timmons for the foundations

To Art Blakey and Ray Bryant for a great fifteenth birthday

To the House of Chan for Lobster Toishan

To the Palm Cafe for $40 lobsters

To Libby Titus, who can't make a left-hand turn

To Carly Simon for being the Jackie Onassis of rock

To Robert Klane for "Where's Poppa" and inspiration

To Walter Beck for delaying the book for three months by being a concerned neighbor

To Bob Cato and John Berg for allowing me to be painted by Norman Rockwell, photographed by Richard Avedon, made up by Dick Smith, and choreographed by Horn-Griner

To Ben Edmonds for tagging along for three years to see that it all worked (did it?)

To Linda, who is too true to be good

To everyone and anybody I forgot, thank you and tuff shit!

Allie

Contents

	Introduckshun	13
	Preamble: Roots	15
1	Teenage Hustling	21
2	How Does It Feel?	49
3	Kooper Sessions	75
4	Life with the Jewish Beatles	83
5	If You're Going to California, Wear Some Brains in Your Head	137
6	Bloodstains on the Keyboard or What to Call Your New Band	155
7	Up against the Expense Account	181
8	I Stand Accused and Other Adventures: A Tale of Two Albums	193
9	Zoot Sims, Shuggie Otis, Don Ellis, a Manager, and the End of an Era	211
10	Loose Ends, Rolling Stones, Folk Singers, and the Boy Who Ate Dog Food	225
	Discography	245
	Index	247

Foreword

BE: The traditional role of the co-writer has been that of a professional supplying his skills to create the illusion that his other half, who in real life might have trouble composing a postcard, is a competent and occasionally even intelligent writer. I'm delighted to be able to report that the situation with Al Kooper couldn't have been further from that stereotype, a fact which unquestionably aided in the preservation of my mental and physical well-being through the sixteen months it took to slap this masterpiece together. These are Al Kooper's stories, and they are recounted in his own words; the project was by conscious design anti-slick. My function was to keep Al on the track and make sure that his reminiscences were appropriately fleshed-out; apart from that, I changed as little as possible. When I had something to add—information, perspective or an opinion for which I alone should be held responsible—I did so in the form this introduction takes. Beyond that, you're one-on-one with Al Kooper. Good luck.

Ben Edmonds, March 1976

Forget everything you ever read or heard about Al Kooper.

PHOTO: DORENE LAUER

Introduckshun

Over the years, I have endured hundreds of interviews when I knew the wrong questions were being asked. This book is a chance to answer all the questions that are invariably left out, as well as answer the most-asked questions in detail.

This is my eighteenth year in the music business. Ten of those years stand out in retrospect as being gloriously exciting: 1959–1969. In this book, Ben Edmonds and I have attempted to allow the reader a glimpse of what it is like to build a career in the music business from scratch in New York, circa the dawn of the sixties.

I am not an altogether serious person. Nor is my book an altogether serious documentation. It's all the *truth*, mind you, but if I had taken myself seriously while it was all happening, I doubt I would be here today to recall it.

Whenever my memory began to dull, Ben Edmonds would whip out his trusty cassette recorder and ask the questions that would put me back on the track and force me to recall things I hadn't thought of in more than a decade. Piecing together tapes, photos, and scraps of paper, we spent four years constructing and rewriting. The final editing by Michaela Hamilton was the icing on the cake for us.

I have taken the liberty of leaving out situations that I believe would hurt people's feelings or cause them problems. I have also left out the things *I* consider pointless in a book of this sort; *i.e.* where I was born, when my parents met, etc. This is rock 'n' roll, and there is no room on board for that stuff here.

14 | Introduckshun

If you want to enlighten yourself with a few facts you might not glean elsewhere and have some fun while doing it, then read on. That is the *only* purpose of this book.

Thanks to Ben Edmonds for helping it all to make sense.

Thanks to Alice Ochs, Columbia Records, and Jim Marshall for saving me thousands of words with their fine photos.

Thanks to Cheryl Houston for typing it all up.

Thanks to my folks for making me.

Have a nice trip.

Al Kooper, March 1976

Preamble: Roots

New York City, you're a woman
Cold hearted bitch ought to be your name
You ain't never loved anybody,
But I'm drawn to you like a moth to flame

—"New York City (You're a Woman)"

© 1971, Sea-Lark Enterprises, Inc. and Joans Bones Music Publishing Inc. (subsidiaries of A. Schroeder International Ltd.) 25 W. 56th St., New York, N.Y. 10019. Used by permission.

Prior to the invention of California, the uncontested center of the music industry universe was a five-block stretch of Broadway in New York City. Three buildings in particular, 1619, 1650, and 1697, summed it all up. Like three octogenarians in a rock 'n' roll rest home, they assume very distinct personalities once you've started them telling their stories of the faces they've seen and the times they've endured.

1619 Broadway (at Forty-eighth Street), more commonly known as the Brill Building, is the youngest of the three, having been constructed in 1931. It was the first of the three, however, to gamble on showbiz by painting ASCAP and BMI on its opaque glass doors instead of MD or DDS. The inherent Jewish/Italian balance was not disturbed by this changeover; the fate of those entering the building was merely transposed from healing to stealing.

The Brill Building stands against a fairly standard New York backdrop of camera stores and record shops that have been going out of business since they opened. (One of the most lucrative ventures in this particular neighborhood is painting Going Out of Business signs.) To the right of the entranceway you can't miss a gnarled specimen of humanity astride a fire hydrant (his only visible means of support). This is the notorious Broadway Larry, the unofficial doorman of the Brill Building and one of the most outrageous characters in all of New York. He's been standing out in front with his shopping bag and unshaven face for as long as anybody can remember, assailing random passersby with an x-rated stream of abuse. When long hair first came into vogue, aspiring hippies were subject to an extra helping of his verbal shit-rain. But the guy's charm was that he so obviously considered *anybody* to be deserving of his hostility. Some of his best victims were immaculately-dressed corporation executives, who'd turn twelve shades of purple when dropped in their tracks by a loud "hey asshole!" from the lips of my man. A great guy, Broadway Larry; a credit to his race.

Once inside, don't be deceived by 1619's ordinary appearance; the Brill Building commanded an impressive clientele that remained faithful through every opportunity to move uptown.

It was here that Elvis Presley's publishing interests were looked after, and where the entire Southern rockabilly scene came to pick up its weekly allowance checks. It was the base of operations of the Goodman family, who handled the Arc publishing empire, which encompassed the likes of Jimmy Reed, Muddy Waters, Willy Dixon, Chuck Berry, Howling Wolf, and nearly every other Chicago blues singer of note. (Arc's fortunes, unlike so much of the other fifties' musical activity, remained unaffected by the renaissance of the sixties. Every white blues-based band, from the Beatles and the Rolling Stones on down, still came to Arc for their cultural authenticity.) Bobby Darin, Don Kirshner, Perry Como, and Frank Sinatra were once just faces in the 1619 hallway crowd. Jerry Lieber and Mike Stoller, the Hardy Boys of rock 'n' roll songwriting, set up shop here and ground out "Young Blood," "Black Denim Trousers and Motorcycle Boots," "Hound Dog," and a good piece of the foundation upon which rock was built.

When Bob Dylan, the Beatles, and others changed the attitude of the music business in 1964, the new messiahs took space in 1650, not wishing to be associated with bygone eras. Nashville went big business, pulling its interests southward. Little by little 1619's charisma faded. As of this writing, the Brill Building is only one-third occupied. The superintendent of the building for the past twenty-five years, Mike Mihok, informed me that the film business is now the building's major source of tenant revenue. *Sic transit gloria mundi.*

•

Though 1650 boasted a Broadway address, its entrance was actually on Fifty-first Street, between Broadway and Seventh Avenue, the building having been erected in 1922, when musicians were still being asked to use the side door. In contrast to the relative seediness of the Brill Building neighborhood, 1650 is on the perimeter of the theater-hotel district.

In 1945, the building changed hands, and the new owners had the foresight to renovate it for the coming musical onslaught. The new music business wasn't buying the shirt-and-tie ambience of the Brill Building. And it was necessary for 1650, like so many of its tenants, to maintain a facade of youth. The rents were cheaper than at 1619, the restrictions virtually none, rendering it possible for almost *anyone* to obtain office space if they had a speed-rap capable of clubbing the rental agent into submission. Many did. It was as if the landlord were some kind of desperate Statue of Liberty imploring, *"Give me your tired, your poor, and pay the fucking rent on time ... please! I need the business!"*

And "the business" he got. Soon 1650 hosted a wide-ranging collection of hustlers and would-be music moguls who didn't have the credentials the Brill Building required and therefore had to establish an alternative order. 1650 was not a place in which to rest on your laurels, it was a place to earn them, and the kind of tension created by people hungry for success gave the building an electricity that immediately distinguished it from 1619.

Aldon Music, the hottest song-publishing concern of the early sixties, dominated 1650's action. The product of Al Nevins, a performer (The Three Suns) and writer ("Twilight Time"), and Don Kirshner, whose television rock programming has established him as a mainstay of the seventies, this company seemed to have the top of the charts padlocked until the Beatles finally intervened. Carole King, Jerry Goffin, Barry Mann, Cynthia Weill, Neil Sedaka, Howie Greenfield, Dee Ervin, and numerous others competed for space at Aldon's piano, on which to compose the hits that would monopolize the airwaves. Though the late George Goldner seldom receives the credit due him, he made records while in residence here that had as much to do with defining the New York black sound as did Ahmet Ertegun over at Atlantic Records. Alan Freed, who coined the phrase rock 'n' roll and is the father of the art form as we know it, maintained an office here, run by his manager, Jack Hook. (For the sake of history, it is interesting to note that Alan Freed's son, Lance, heads up the publishing wing of A & M records, and that George Goldner's daughter, Linda, was married to contemporary super-producer Richard Perry and has produced several records herself.) Until he contracted California fever, Neil Diamond occupied a cubicle at 1650. Leo Rogers, who managed the Royal Teens, and Aaron Schroeder, who today administers the Barry White Publishing Catalogue, had office space there. It also housed Ray Rand's cooking little venture, Adelphi Studios. These latter three gentlemen all played an important part in my early education, and we'll return to them later.

Of the three buildings, 1650 continues to be the most active. Current tenants include the Isley Brothers, The Queen Booking Corporation (the largest black theatrical agency, handling the likes of Aretha Franklin and Sammy Davis, Jr.) and Charles Rapp (an agent whose name is synonymous with the Catskill treadmill—he gave Lenny Bruce his first abortive break on that circuit.) Above the entrance to the building is a sign bearing the inscription: "1650 Broadway, the best known address in the entertainment field." An exaggeration, perhaps, but not by all that much.

1697 Broadway could have been the place where the adjective *funky* was coined, and certainly remains the definitive explanation of the term. Built in 1907 (my father wasn't built until 1909) and originally called the Hammerstein Building (my father was originally called Kuperschmidt), this was the smallest and craziest of the three. It penetrated the theater district even further than 1650, and sat in a weird neighborhood hybrid of Cadillac and Chevrolet showrooms, office buildings, and respectable hotels. On the east side of Broadway, somebody had picked up the tab for extensive renovation in the form of modern high rises, and formerly ugly residences had been transformed into cute little office buildings. But if you walked one block west to Eighth Avenue you'd find yourself in the middle of Dylan's "desolation row," an area infested with whore houses, sleazy bars, and porno-supermarkets totally beyond renovation or redemption.

The ground floor of 1697 was given over to the CBS TV soundstage from which the "Ed Sullivan Show" used to beam its way into millions of American homes every Sunday night (which is about as far from funky as you can get). Up the stairs and around the corner, however, lurked the specter of rhythm and blues, a festering sore on the face of "white American culture." This building was predominately black, to the extent that the few white people who took up residence almost felt obliged to have at least one R&B hit (e.g., The Tokens, Jewish as the driven snow, who produced a sizable R&B hit in "He's So Fine" by the Chiffons, and later ended up winning a suit against George Harrison, for borrowing more than a few bars from it for his "My Sweet Lord"). Upstairs were countless dance studios, recording facilities (most notably Broadway Recording Studios, now defunct), and rehearsal studios where you'd have to fight for listening space in the hallway when Ray Charles cracked the whip over his big band or James Brown ran his supersweat revue through its paces.

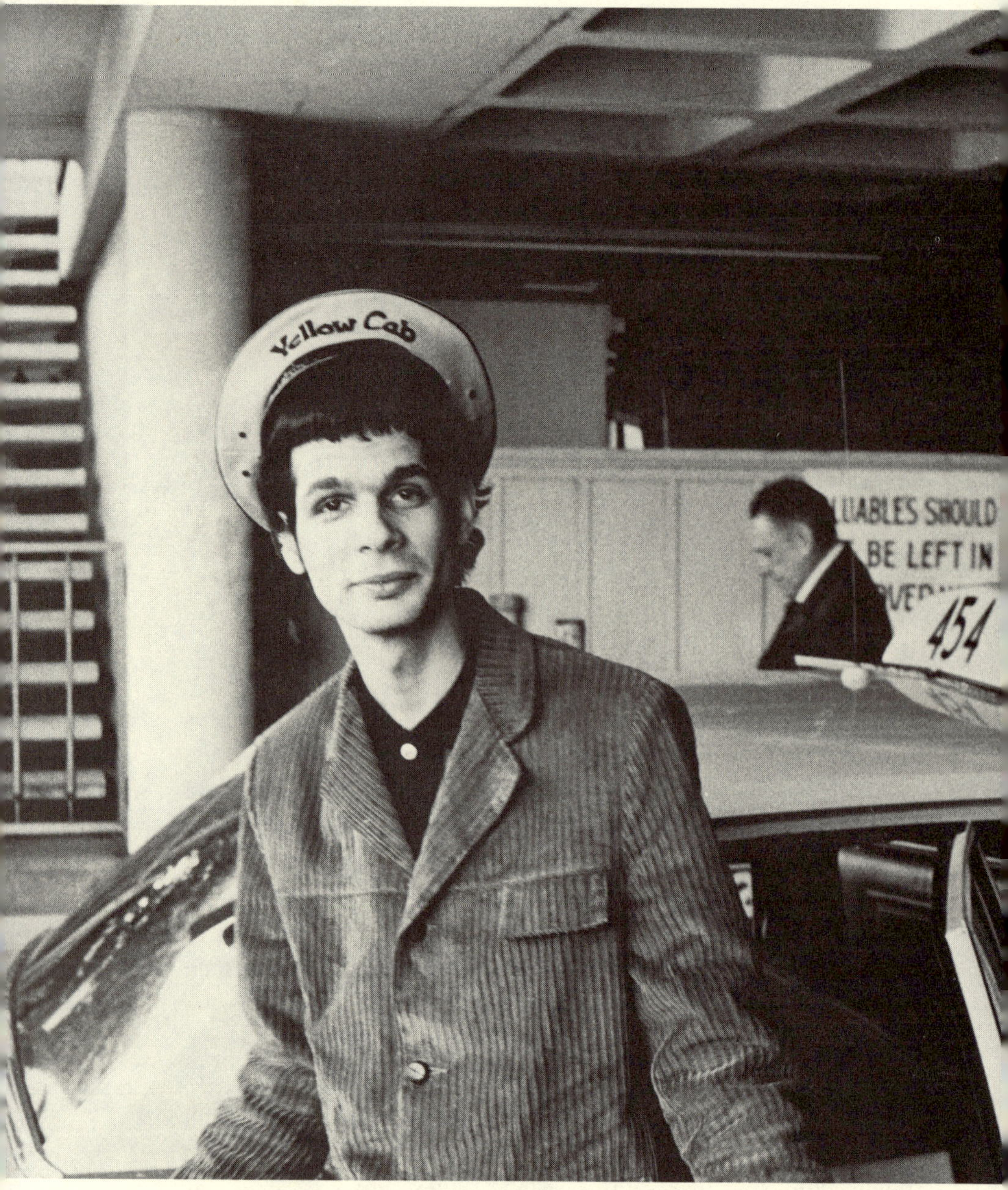
Yellow Cab
LUABLES SHOULD
BE LEFT IN
454

1

Teenage Hustling

I stumbled into the picture in the late fifties at the tender age of thirteen. I'd gone to summer camp with this guy named Danny Schactman, a guitar player with a band that actually had a record out. The record was the original "Baby Talk," which didn't become a hit until Jan & Dean picked it up a couple of years later. As a fledgling guitar "virtuoso," I was fascinated by this apparent stardom and cultivated a friendship with Danny that lasted beyond the summer.

BE: Now you might well find the image of a rock 'n' roll recording star at summer camp a little incongruous. But just as there was a singing group on practically every street corner, there were dozens of equally small-time record companies. Most of the groups and the companies never got off their corners, but having a record out was not that unusual for a kid growing up in New York. Almost like riding bicycles and collecting baseball cards. You can all remember seeing little Ricky Nelson on "Ozzie and Harriet," singing the number-one hit in the nation at his school dance after being bailed out of some routine domestic disaster by Ozzie's sound advice. Also, the fact that your average thirteen-year-old can barely even spell business, let alone deal with it, sometimes made it easier to get work. Child labor has always been cheap.

Shortly before I was due to be inducted into the eighth grade, I spent a week at Danny's house in Brooklyn. One day, we journeyed to his manager's office at 1650 Broadway. Leo Rogers was a man in his middle fifties who discovered and managed some of the more dubious oneshot wonders of that time. Leo subscribed to the underhanded style of doing business, and there were always students and stooges at his feet hoping to pick up the finer points of his locally legendary style. There was also an abundance of kids in my situation, dying for a chance to do *anything* for the experience it offered. We knew we were being ripped off, but our financial interests at such a formative age were strictly secondary.

I was auditioned as a guitar player.

"Okay, kid," Leo said, "show us your stuff."

I wailed out reasonable facsimiles of "Rumble" and "Rawhide" on my Sears Roebuck special. To my surprise, it made 'em smile. (Later, I found out why they were smiling.) I was offered a job for that very night, backing a group called the Casuals who had just scored with the song "So Tough." Since I was staying at Danny's that week, I accepted. My parents would never have to know that their underage darling was consorting with hardened musicians long after he should have been home safely in bed. A group of us piled into a car and headed for the scene of the crime, a high school gym somewhere on Long Island.

Even though my experience consisted mainly of playing along to the radio and Chuck Berry records, the gig was easy. In those days, the average set ran about twenty minutes. You'd play your hit, and whatever else was popular at the time (*i.e.* whatever songs the band happened to know.)

BE: Quite a contrast to what happened a generation later, when groups like the Grateful Dead were known to play for days at a time, and concerts seemed to have become feats of physical endurance.

I had a cursory knowledge of the chords to the hits of the moment, so someone would just call out the key and we'd be off. Before the show you'd get an iridescent jacket and a bow tie (which never fit, not that it mattered), and the rest was pretty automatic. At the end of the evening, you might pick up fifteen dollars for your efforts. It seemed like heaven.

Thus ended any pretense I might have had about leading a normal existence. From then on, whenever I had money in my pocket I'd become the phantom of 1650. Hanging out at Rogers' office promised an education more useful than anything junior high was offering, and when you don't know nothing you've got plenty to learn. If I was lucky enough to be hanging around at the right time, I might even get a shot at earning my subway fare back home for the week. Which is how I came to join the Royal Teens.

•

The Royal Teens (also managed by Leo Rogers) had scored one national smash with a cute little novelty item called "Short Shorts." One day I happened to be in the office when the call went out for a guitar player. The only problem was that I wasn't staying at Danny Schactman's house that weekend, and so my parents had to be brought into the negotiations. I was fourteen years old at the time. Protective animals by nature, my folks demanded an audience with Rogers. Leo explained to them that the job was in Monticello, a four-and-a-half hour drive from the city, and that he'd assure my safety by personally driving me home. Thus assuaged, my parents sanctioned the donning of the iridescent jacket and bow tie, a move destined to fill them with remorse for many years to come.

By the time we finished up in Monticello it was one in the morning, which already put the promised hour of my safe return well out of reach. We piled into Leo's car, and I fell sound asleep. I awoke at 4:00 A.M. to find myself surrounded by five snoring faces, and the car pulled off the road in a cornfield.

I shook Leo awake (he was the only one old enough to drive), and without a word he turned the key in the ignition and headed toward home as if he was on automatic pilot. God knows what he was really on! When I woke up again it was 5:30 A.M. and I was being dropped off in the heart of Manhattan, miles from my doorstep. Nothing to do now but phone the folks and brace yourself.

"Hi," I said as casually as you can when you know you've already been tried and convicted. "We just got back into town and I guess I'll be getting a subway."

"Subway! Where's Leo Rogers?"

"Oh, he's gone home."

For the next two minutes there was nothing at the other end of the line but the sound of two mature adults going completely berserk. When they regained partial control of their faculties, I was ordered to get my little ass into a Queens-bound taxicab. Their treat.

This is a scene that I've never been able to forget: Sitting in the back of that taxicab in my oversized iridescent blue and black jacket, with my Sears guitar and cheezy little amp in the seat beside me, watching the first sunrise I'd ever seen against the New York skyline. Then pulling up in front of our house in Queens one step ahead of the milktruck. Passing my father on the front walk; he on his way to his job, me just returning from mine. And that *look on his face* as he hurried by me, as if an inner voice was telling him, "Your son was abducted by Martians carrying electric guitars. He'll never be the same again." It would have made a perfect portrait for *Rock Dreams*.

This, of course, ended my officially endorsed career as a musician. Leo Rogers was shitlisted, and from then on I was forced to operate undercover. The capper to the incident was that I didn't get paid for the gig! It turned out to be my "audition" for the Royal Teens.

•

I continued my clandestine romance with rock 'n' roll as a member of the Royal Teens. Whenever a job would pop up, I'd have to invent a reason to be staying overnight at a friend's. I'd be playing in Boston, and my parents would be convinced that I was only around the corner. With an intricate network of comrades covering my tracks, the deceptions usually worked.

Still, my parents must have thought it odd that their son was so often preoccupied staying overnight with the guys.

In those days there were no John Denver albums to take home and share with your folks. Rock 'n' roll was the line of division, and the life-style attached to it had to be kept undercover. I embraced it all: black leather jacket (mine was actually brown; one of many such concessions), rolled-up sleeves, greasy hair, and engineer's boots. I would've had sideburns if I could've grown them.

Naturally my parents weren't buying any of this, so I was forced to keep a stash of contraband clothing in a friend's garage. I'd wake up in the morning and get dressed, bid my parents goodbye, and head directly for the friend's house, where I'd *really* get dressed for school. On more than one occasion, my mother would "happen" to be driving by the bus stop, would spot me dressed illegally and bust me. I think she made a point of driving that route every morning. But her plan wasn't enough to stop me; I smuggled my clothes into school and changed every morning in the bathroom. Super-Punk!

I worked hard at an aura of toughness, but actually faced with a fight, I wouldn't have lasted long enough to take a punch. Luckily, being a musician had its advantages. "The bad guys know us and they leave us alone" is the way Brian Wilson put it in "I Get Around," [*] and that's pretty much the way it was. If I didn't push the tough-guy pose too far, I'd never get called on it. This explains how I managed to pass through New York City public schools with my life support systems intact.

The one time I couldn't avoid a fight, neither my mouth nor my guitar could've saved me. I was on my way home from a gig in one of New York's innumerable lousy neighborhoods, and had all the arrogance beaten out of me by three black dudes in a deserted subway station. I'd recently begun an infatuation with black music, and the beating was as much psychic as physical.

---

[*] "I Get Around" words and music by Brian Wilson © 1964 Irving Music Inc. All rights reserved. International copyright secured.

"Hey," I kept wanting to scream, "if you knew how much I liked Jimmy Reed, would you do this to me?" You bet your ass, we would, Honkey!

•

To become an accepted member of the band's inner circle, you had to suffer an initiation as the butt of many practical jokes. State of the art was the put-on. Like we'd be driving home from a job, and one of the guys would turn and say, "Hey, let's be honest, fellas." That was the tipoff to the routine; the only one who wasn't hip to it was the intended mark. "How many times a week do you jerk off?" Like they're in the habit of unlocking their most dreaded secrets just to kill some time on a drive back from a gig.

Each guy would pick a number and do his own confessional. "Now come on, you gotta be really honest, that's the whole point of this," doing a straight-face setup on the poor schmuck. So you'd blurt out your awful truth, and they'd take it every bit as seriously as they'd taken their fabrications. Then they'd let you sit for a couple of hours, feeling good about the bond of intimacy you'd created, until one of them would turn and casually say, "You know that thing we did back there about jerking off? Well, we all made up our answers." You couldn't do anything except sit there red-faced, in a puddle, thinking "Oh shit" over and over again the rest of the way home.

Another favorite on the mental-cruelty hit parade was a game called "Who's the Star This Week?" One of the guys would pop the question in the dressing room, well within earshot of the newest member, who'd go for the bait immediately. "Well, every week," we'd explain, "one of us gets to be the star and can tell everyone else in the band what to do. That means Leo, too. Like last week, Al was the star, and he had Leo shine his shoes right before he went on stage. Leo can't ever be the star, 'cuz he's the manager and that means he's always the star. That's why we set up the star system."

Of course it was always the new chump's turn to be the star, and you could see him swell up with his imagined authority. When Leo ambled into the room, the kid would unknowingly deliver the punch line. "Hey, Leo," he'd command, "bend over and kiss my ass before I go on tonight!"

Leo would stand there in total disbelief, suddenly developing severe Parkinson's disease and a suntan that Coppertone Q-T couldn't have matched for acceleration. When all the blood reached his brain, the top of his skull would blow off. "What the fuck izza matter wichoo," he'd scream. The kid would usually run for the nearest corner with his tenor sax between his legs.

When faced with an interview or the presence of somebody we didn't like, we had a bit where we'd jabber in mock Chinese. When a normal person (in those days we called them squares) is confronted with a number of potentially dangerous adolescents ranting in tongues, his first impulse is to be someplace else. Which was precisely the point. It was like a square alert, a defense against a world none of us felt much a part of when we put on those iridescent jackets. But squares were such easy targets that we only used these tactics in self-defense.

There were times when cheap laffs were the only remuneration we could expect. I was lucky to average $10 a night. So when the Royal Teens' comet showed signs of cooling off, I took my ass elsewhere; to 1697 Broadway and the office of Jim Gribble.

·

Though he never seemed to be a manager in any active sense of the word, Jim Gribble manipulated the fortunes of some of the biggest local do-wop heroes, among them the Passions ("Just To Be With You") and the Mystics ("Hush-A-Bye"). He was an imposing figure—a hefty 6-4 and 250 pounds—and a slow, deliberate talker.

BE: He could be played in the movie by John Wayne.

Contrasting the authoritarian Rogers attitude, he was incredibly patient and seemed to take a genuine interest in his musicians, though it was perfectly understood that his patience would be suitably rewarded if they happened to make it big.

Jim Gribble was never as successful as Leo Rogers, most

likely because he lacked that razor-sharp killer instinct, but his office certainly offered more possibilities. At the ripe old age of sixteen I was writing songs and hustling my way into whatever sessions I could, and Gribble's office provided a much more receptive atmosphere in which to peddle my flesh. Gribble, you see, was always very kind-hearted about your exploitation. He'd throw a fast five bucks your way for banging out a few tunes at one of his several daily auditions, or sometimes just when you looked like you needed it.

The point of connection at Gribble's was a kid about my age named Stan Vincent, who did whatever needed to be done, from emptying ashtrays to arranging and sometimes even producing a session. He didn't always get credit for his studio tasks, but I zeroed in on his position as exactly what I was looking for myself. Having youth and musical aspirations in common, it was natural that we became friends. And by hanging out with him, I was assured of a bit of work here and there. It's even conceivable that in the course of our relationship we taught each other a thing or two. Stan later went on to write and produce "Ooo Child" by the Five Stairsteps, one of my favorite singles.

I'd get out of school at noon and race to Gribble's office. (The official schoolday didn't end at noon, but *mine* did. We all know rock 'n' roll doesn't encourage an avid interest in formal education.) I'd arrive and the place would look like an unemployment office in the wake of one of Richard Nixon's economic programs. There'd be people crowding the office and spilling out into the hall, each one with a hustle he hoped was better than the one that hadn't worked out for him the week before. Guys with guitars. Guys with songs. Guys with pretty faces and no talent. Guys with nothing going for them but their mouths.

You were in competition for everything, from your seat in the outer office to your gig at the afternoon's demo session, and the point of the game was to make yourself as conspicuously available as possible. The oldest profession in the world. It didn't matter that you ran the risk of making the same nothing for playing your dick off at a session that you could just as easily make by sitting at home watching the Knicks game; what we were all grasping at was the opportunity for *involvement*. My philosophy was that you couldn't afford the luxury of trying to be in the right place in the right time. You had to try and be *every* place at *every* time, and hope that you might wind up anyplace at all. It was a bitch to keep up with, but eventually it worked.

One of Gribble's pet regulars was Phil Anastasia, a good-looking smoothie from a rugged Italian background, and Gribble was determined to do a Fabian on him.

BE: "Doing a Fabian" was a much-favored music business pastime of the late fifties. It consisted of finding a kid with a face and then steering clear of any discussion to do with talent. The face would cut a record—usually with all the technical make-up necessary to hide the blemishes—that was criminally calculated to appeal to indiscriminate teenage tastes. Then, promoting the face heavily, the record company might be lucky enough to squeeze out one or two profitable records before the inevitable happened and the face found himself back at the gas station or beefcake movie circuit from whence he had come.

This ploy was especially beloved of music businessmen in New York and Philadelphia in those days, even more so than it is in England today. The myriad TV stars who have been pushed into recording studios, along with Fabian's return as a serious actor, have antiquated the term "doing a Fabian." However, the practice continues.

For reasons that still haven't caught up with me, Gribble selected one of my songs to be the vehicle that would carry Phil Anastasia to his appointment with destiny. (Maybe they figured that if the record was going to sell to people with no taste, it would be to their advantage to have somebody with no taste compose it.)

It wasn't long before I was able to wave vinyl proof-positive of my flowering success in the faces of all those who'd doubted my gift: "My Kind of Love" by Anastasia on Laurie Records.

BE: Laurie was the label Dion & the Belmonts recorded for, so add an automatic two points for teen prestige.

To explain the song's limited success, you need only consider its first verse: "When you hold my hand/I understand/Oh yeah, that's my kind of love." * After that the song kind of petered out lyrically, but you got the idea. I think Anastasia's parents and my parents purchased the only copies, then tucked them away where neighbors couldn't see them and ask to have them played. The record might not've been good, but it was real. The kid now had credentials as a songwriter.

•

Jim Gribble died shortly thereafter, a fate most of his groups shared with him around this time. I went to his funeral; it was ill-attended and depressing. Jim Gribble was a good man, one of the few who made sure that his door was always open to untested talent. For that, even the losers should line up to offer thanks.

Following Gribble's death, I drifted back to 1650. In the building was a company that Dick Clark had owned, called Sea Lark. (C-lark, get it?) It was a music publishing company that owned a few hit copyrights, among them "16 Candles" and "At the Hop." The company was purchased by a moderately successful songwriter named Aaron Schroeder ("Good Luck Charm," "Stuck on You"), who kept the company alive through its formative stages by channeling his own writing into it. He was looking for staff writers at the time I happened to be in need of a publishing home, so right away it seemed like a mutually agreeable arrangement. Papers to that effect were quickly passed.

Still intoxicated by the sweet non-success of "My Kind of Love," I came armed with a full repertoire of songs equally terrible. I guess Schroeder was really desperate to fill his catalogue, because the shuffling of papers was about the only action these songs ever saw. Most of them now qualify as

---

* © 1960 January Music Corporation (a subsidiary of A. Schroeder International Ltd.) 25 W. 56th St., New York, N.Y. 10019. Used by permission.

blackmail items (for *both* of us). Then one day in math class—the only time I showed up for the entire term—I was moved to write an incisive piece of social commentary lampooning the Vic Tanny gym chain. I cut a demo of it with a couple of friends and played it for Schroeder. Knowing that all the world loves a novelty for at least five minutes, he snapped it up for the record company he was about to launch.

With little deliberation and no argument, it was decided that my voice was unsuited to this particular gem. So Leo DeLyon, a comedian who did voice-overs for cartoons and was even rumored to have been the voice of Popeye, was summoned to render the lead vocal. And in 1961, Musicor Records was born with a single 45 release "Sick Manny's Gym," by Leo DeLyon & the Musclemen (the Aristocats, my hometown local band).

BE: If Vic Tanny could've seen the muscleman who was playing guitar on this session, he would've gone into the shoe business!

The flip side was "Plunkin," an instrumental by the Musclemen/Aristocats.

BE: All thru his Royal Teens and other early hustling associations Al maintained this band with a bunch of neighborhood chums. They played church dances, temple celebrations, and school functions—the kind of healthy operation that parents of junior-high brats sponsor every day of the week. Besides, it meant that the parents could take turns chauffeuring the kids back and forth from their jobs, thereby keeping an eye on the little bastards.

Unlike the Anastasia record, an attempt was made to promote this one. Ads were taken out in the trades, DJs were hyped. We actually heard it on the radio a couple of times, which made for instant visions of sumptuous royalty statements and trips to Acapulco. Until we realized that after the first time we heard it, no one got around to playing the record again. Oh well, strike four.

One Saturday morning with nothing better to do, I hopped a subway into the city to see if I could scrounge up a session. People seldom came in on weekends, but I stopped by 1650 to check the offices anyway. Schroeder happened to be in, and welcomed my company. He had a kid coming in to audition for his label—a friend of a friend from Rockville(!), Connecticut. He wanted my opinion, something I've never been known to be at a loss for, and invited me to stick around.

In walks this dude in a salt and pepper jacket, heavily greased-down DA, and white bucks. Three dressing schools tied together; very strange. The creature sat down at the piano and proceeded to mesmerize us for two uninterrupted hours with his incredible songs and bizarre voice. He was an original, and the impact on me was like hearing black church music for the first time. But one of the mightiest music business ordinances forbids you to *ever* give yourself away, so Schroeder and I did our utmost to refrain from hailing him as the unique talent he was. After the kid split, Schroeder nonchalantly asked me what I thought.

"What could anyone think," I said, knowing that we both knew the answer perfectly well. "Sign the motherfucker."

"Should we change his name?" Shroeder asked.

"Don't make no difference what you call him," I answered. "Gene Pitney is a star!"

My analysis was proven correct, with no small thanks to the energies of Aaron Schroeder. He cleared out all the legal deadwood around Pitney, then signed him to a contract so thorough that it might've included bathroom privileges. Gene even moved into Schroeder's apartment, and his campaign was carefully and intelligently planned.

BE: This was called "grooming" as opposed to "doing a Fabian." The difference was undeniable talent.

The first step was to cut rough demos of all Gene's material, some of which I played on (and a few of which eventually found

The young Aristo-Cats: Bob Tannenbaum, Joe Heyman, Eric Krackow, and the Kid. PHOTO: LOU KRACKOW.

The older Aristo-Cats: Jerry Cohen, Eric Krackow, Joe Heyman, and the Kid in a sharkskin suit. PHOTO: JUDY KOOPER.

their way into circulation disguised as real records). When Schroeder discovered that nearly every record company enthusiastically seconded his high estimation of Pitney's worth, he resolved to use him to *establish* Musicor Records. It was reassuring to know that the fate of the company wasn't riding on *my* record anymore.

Though Pitney didn't take off until "Town Without Pity," his name was beginning to ring a few bells, thanks to Schroeder's boundless hustle. He placed choice Pitney material with classy customers: "He's a Rebel" by the Crystals, "Hello Marylou" by Ricky Nelson, "Today's Teardrops" by Roy Orbison, and "Rubber Ball" by Bobby Vee. Before Pitney's own records could claim the power to make teenage hearts flutter, the rest of the industry could see it coming. And when the powers-that-be accept an inevitability, it takes an act of God to prevent it (witness Bruce Springsteen!).

Soon Phil Spector was cutting sides with Gene. Then it was Burt Bacharach (whom Schroeder also spotted early-on). Aaron had an eye for good combinations, a knack you can acquire only by a thorough understanding of the artist you're dealing with and the marketplace in which his art will be peddled. If you look hard enough, you'll even find a couple of Al Kooper originals buried on early Pitney albums, which was as expedient a move as any of the others Schroeder was making. He produced Pitney's albums and he published my songs, so the Sea-Lark godfather could keep all his children happy with a single stroke.

Pitney's influence on me was more pervasive than I realized. We became friends and spent a healthy amount of time in each other's company. Unconsciously, I assimilated aspects of his style. I started to sing like him. I started to play the piano like him. I started to write songs that only he could have inspired. I was still a lump of clay in search of a benevolent pair of hands, and his proved to be strong and agreeable to my ends. To this day, I still possess a few Gene Pitney habits that've never been broken; subtle colorings that still show up on my canvases. As a point of information, "Just One Smile," the Randy Newman song on the first Blood, Sweat & Tears album, originated on an old

Pitney LP. Newman, you see, was at that time *also* contracted to Schroeder as a songwriter.

I, meanwhile, had committed a drastic error in judgment by enrolling as a music major at the University of Bridgeport. I did it partially to appease my parents, who had yet to be convinced that my fixation with the music business was anything but a collision course with an unsavory fate or (at best) a slowly passing fancy. I viewed college as an opportunity to fill in the details of my technical musical knowledge. If I was gonna be a bum, I was gonna be a bum who would read and write music.

I should've guessed that higher education was not to play a part in my future when I discovered I couldn't major in either of the instruments I played. I had the feel, but not the fingers, required of a piano major; and the concept of a guitar major had never occurred to the faculty, so our rock 'n' roll animal wound up majoring in bass fiddle.

To keep in touch with the outside world (and to make sure I had enough money to buy magazines and records), I would write ghost arrangements in my spare time.

BE: Ghost arrangers are from the same basic stock as ghost writers. When an arranger takes on more than he can chew, he will occasionally farm out some of the overload to preserve his reputation as a man who gets things done. No one but the arranger himself is aware of this deception, and he can pull it off because there will always be talented people available whose hunger outweighs their ego.

I could usually pick up an extra two or three hundred dollars by driving into New York City to pick up the songs on a Monday and returning the finished arrangements on Thursday. Far as I could tell, I learned more from this than from any course I was taking at the time, and the comparative enormity of this task made it a cinch for me to breeze through my homework.

One assignment for music theory class included a simple four-part Bach chorale, with one missing part that the student was to fill in. Took me about eight seconds; it was so trivial compared to the ghost writing. When homework was handed back a few days later, though, mine was returned covered with red marks. After suffering through hours of uninspired classes and being taught page after page of extraneous information I knew I would never use, this was the ultimate insult.

When class was dismissed, I approached the professor's desk and asked him why he'd decorated my homework so colorfully. Then I sat down at the classroom piano and played my version of Bach for him.

"It's not the way Bach would have written it," he said.

"Sir, I'm no expert in reincarnation," I said, "but, taking an educated guess, I would say that I am probably not Bach—just a student trying to enrich his knowledge in an effort to bolster his *creativity*."

The teacher looked up at me for the first time in the conversation. "Mr. Kooper," he said, "you must first learn the rules before you can break them."

This astonished me.

"Well, sir," I replied, "now that I have divined your teaching philosophy, I think it's safe to say that you will never see this face in your fucked-up classroom again."

And he never did.

•

I tried to back out of the whole college thing gracefully at the six-month point, but my parents, in a last-ditch effort to salvage their investment, dragged a commitment out of me to see the full year through.

I made the concession to stay, but nothing was said about *studying*. So I didn't. I just maintained a residence in the dorm and wrote free-lance arrangements for people in New York, while my classmates fought the typical sixties paranoia that if they didn't make it in college, they were doomed to sweep bus station floors for the rest of eternity. I also put together an eccentric little student combo to keep my performing chops in order.

Eventually I got so bored that I even performed manual labor at the local pizzeria, where I had the opportunity to stack the jukebox with my own material. I went so far as to have some of my own demos pressed into 45s, and thus became the "Artist of the Week" on the pizzeria Seeburg. Al Kooper, the Jukebox King of Bridgeport. That and a goatee were my only tangible college accomplishments. If you wanna teach music to a bunch of simps who wanna teach music to a bunch of simps, then studying music in college is just what the doctor ordered. All the universities in the world couldn't tell you as much about music as one tour with a Dick Clark Caravan of Stars show!

Anyway, it was nobody's loss when I finally packed it in and went home. I made yet another deal with my folks: if by the end of one year in the music business I hadn't achieved anything significant, I'd return to college. I didn't have the slightest intention of honoring my end of the bargain, of course, but it gave me at least temporarily the kind of freedom I was looking for.

•

My first brush with gainful employment in the real world was as a stockboy in the record department of one of New York's immense department store nightmares. My memory of this tenure is hazy, but I seem to recall that carting Christmas inventory up from the basement for one hellish week cured me of any notions I might've had about the value of honest labor. I still blanch at the sight of a Ray Coniff's Christmas Favorites album.

My next foray into the business world was an out-and-out Kooper scam, the first in a long line. I'd mastered the basics of a few instruments, and while I wasn't exactly the picture of grace on any of them, through the magic process of overdubbing (recording in tandem from one machine to another) I could turn out a record all by myself. This was a cheap way to make demos of the songs I wrote; they were acceptable as long as you didn't actually *listen* to them.

Backed by an extensive catalogue of limited skills, I convinced Ray Rand of Adelphi Studios at 1650 to donate space in his stockroom for my use as an office. The scheme was that I would solicit publishers to hire me for the purpose of producing their song demos. For a package price of ninety dollars a song, I'd give them a vocalist and a full rhythm section playing an arrangement, with all the studio time provided for. This was quite a bargain, as long as nobody got wise to the fact that this one scrawny Jewish kid was playing everything, and poorly at that.

So, in January of 1963, with one-hundred business cards and printed statements to prove that I was serious, Ko-op Productions came into being. Also included in my arrangement with Ray Rand was responsibility for sweeping the studio floor at day's end. This task earned me the title "apprentice engineer."

At first, I did a lot of sweeping. When the boss went home, however, the engineers would loosen up and occasionally impart a few tricks of their trade. In this way, I picked up an introduction to the art of engineering, and promptly used that knowledge to deceive my employers whenever possible. Left to my own devices, I'd make a demo of *my* current song, exhausting countless hours of studio time that somehow never showed up in the log books.

Finally the Ko-op bait landed someone—an oldline publisher who sent down music sheets to three songs he needed immediate demos of. A paying customer! I slaved for three days, and though the outcome was every bit as crude as you might imagine, I felt like Phil Spector when the demos were sent to the publisher for his approval. When he heard them, however, he let out a shriek that is reported to have stopped traffic as far away as Newark. And the next day he was in the studio himself, re-cutting the songs with authentic musicians. My cover was blown, and I was back to soliciting the halls of 1650.

•

While I was hustling my unemployed ass one day, a publisher named Hal Webman suggested that I might work well with a pair of lyricists he had under contract. Bob Brass and Irwin Levine had already enjoyed a couple of hits—"A Thing of the Past" by The Shirelles and "Little Lonely One" by The Jarmells—but they needed a bona fide musician to work with.

Bona fide? I'm sure that if they asked the publisher from the Ko-op debacle to estimate my musical worth, he'd have given them a whole different set of adjectives. I was always one for challenges, however, and took on the task of catching up to their level of professionalism. Ko-op was abandoned and Hal Webman's company, We Three Music, assumed the responsibility of paying me the princely twenty-five dollars a week that Ray Rand and Adelphi Studios had.

The alliance between the three of us was an easy one to forge. Brass and Levine were about three years my senior, had gone to high school together in Union, New Jersey, and had also embraced the let's-dispense-with-college philosophy to take a stab at the music biz. With two hits under their belts they were confident, fairly talented, and Jewishly fearless. My background was reasonably similar, and while my youthful inexperience made me their scapegoat too often for my liking, it was a workable situation that taught me a lot.

Our environment consisted of a little corner in Hal Webman's office where there happened to be a piano, and we wrote "follow-up" songs for a living. In other words, if Bobby Vee had a hit out called "Please Don't Ask about Barbara," we'd compose a ditty called "Don't Mention Martha" for him and it would be in the same key and tempo with roughly the same chord changes. We repeated this process for every hit record that was out. Unfortunately, the hit artists never recorded our follow-ups but, with credit to Hal Webman, they did get the opportunity to *hear* them. There were enough has-beens and carbon copy performers to insure fairly steady action on our songs.

First Keely Smith recorded one (she sang it on the Sullivan show; my folks loved that), then Johnny Thunder (remember "Here We Go Loop-de-Loop"?). None of these were hits, but they kept our names out there and temporarily kept the Christmas inventory off my back.

•

The job was so mechanical that every now and then we'd have to resort to some left-field caper to preserve our collective sanity. I remember once there was a power struggle going on in the office between Webman and his partner, Larry Spier, Jr. I'm not sure that we even knew the details of the conflict, but Hal Webman was the one who signed our paychecks, and so that automatically tipped the scales in his favor.

One night the three of us stayed on to work after the office staff had departed, and a bottle of Scotch was discovered in an unguarded desk drawer. Between the three of us it was emptied in no time at all. It must have been a particularly tough day for me because I had already been diagnosed as a probable ulcer victim, but didn't think twice about downing the Dewar's. All of a sudden we were seized by the inspiration to break down Junior's door.

"Okay," Irwin says, "if we break his door down I'll take a shit on his desk." Really drunk. It became imperative to break the door down, because Brass and I desperately wanted to see Irwin do the dump. Had to have it. So we did the thing like in the movies. The three of us grouped at the far corner of the room and barrelled into the door. The only thing that happened, of course, was that we hurt ourselves.

Then we decided we'd *kick* the door down. First we tried kicking around the handle, three rounds of ten kicks apiece. Again nothing happened. Coming to the conclusion that our heads must have been as thick as the door, we tapped all over it until we ascertained that the middle was the weakest section. It was here that we concentrated our ten-kicks system until the first crack appeared. We collapsed in a drunken pile on the floor, hysterical 'cause we knew it was only a matter of time. We smashed at that fuckin' door with a vengeance; it looked like some crazy animal had attacked it. When we had a big enough hole in the door, I reached in and opened it.

"Okay Irwin, time to do your stuff."

Opting to give his performance in private, Irwin temporarily banished Brass and me from the room. All this time we were convulsed, exercising a level of humor we thought had been left in kindergarten. Irwin emerged five minutes later wearing a self-satisfied grin, and, while fastening his belt, announced, "Boys, I got a TEXAS TWISTER to show you!" The sight of that smoldering pile of excrement was like fitting the last piece in some bizarre jigsaw puzzle. It crippled us.

When the laughter finally subsided, paranoia set in. "Hey," it suddenly occurred to Irwin, "we could get in trouble for this." We immediately decided that it couldn't have been us that had done this horrible thing. In a burst of drunken logic, we took magazines, office supplies, and plants and began scattering them all over the room. "We'll tell 'em that robbers were here."

Right! Ten minutes into our campaign to make it look as though the office had been burglarized, Brass tapped Irwin on the shoulder. "You know, schmuck," he said in an uncharacteristic moment of clear light, "robbers don't shit on desks."

On that note, we decided it would be intelligent to evacuate the premises *pronto*. We killed a few minutes in another office to cover ourselves with an alibi ("But, officer, we couldn't possibly have been at the scene of the crap. We were two floors down talking to John Doe at the time.") As we were leaving the building, we passed the doddering old janitor shuffling out of the elevator talking to himself. "*Jesus,*" he muttered, shaking his head in disbelief, "*they done broke down the door, splinters an' evuhthang!*"

A police car was pulling up as we made our getaway, but the Scotch had numbed our paranoia, and even the appearance of the law couldn't dampen our spirits. "Can you imagine the cops when they find that turd on the desk! Can you imagine the *janitor* finding it!" So we went and treated ourselves to a Chinese dinner at the appropriately named Ho Ho Restaurant.

Over another Scotch aperitif we realized that it would be expedient to call Hal Webman and give him our side of the story first. Okay, we'll draw straws. We took three toothpicks and made one short. Of course, always the scapegoat, I strawed the shortest pick. I stumbled to the pay phone and dialed Hal Webman.

"Hal, we got drunk, we kicked in Junior's door and threw a bunch of things around, we'll pay for all the damage. I think the police are there now, 'cause after we did it the janitor saw it."

"Okay," he says, "I'll take care of it."

Grinning, I hung up the phone and returned to the table. The two of them were in hysterics.

"Al, what did he say when you told him Irwin shit on the desk?"

"I forgot to tell him."

"Call him back," they screamed.

"Do I have—"

"Call him back," they screamed even louder.

I sheepishly made my way back to the phone booth. Busy. Of course it's busy. I tried it again. This time, unfortunately, he answered.

"Hal," I began hesitantly, then hit full stride. "I forgot to mention that Irwin shit on Larry's desk."

Long pause, followed by a disbelieving "He what? . . . oh my God, I'll see you tomorrow." Click.

Early the next morning, Hal called us at home and said that if we'd apologize to Junior as soon as we came in it would square everything; he had already made arrangements to pay for the door in our behalf. I arrived at the office first and said, "Larry, I'm really sorry, you know, we were just drunk and it got out of hand." He said okay. He evidently never got to see the turd. Irwin came in next and did the same. Everything was going fine until Brass's entrance. He took one look at the splintered door and broke into a horse-laugh which transformed Irwin and me into instant hyenas. We almost lost our jobs thanks to Brass's ill-timed outburst. But at least we knew shit from Shinola.

•

I remember getting loaded on reefer my first time. I smoked dope on three separate occasions before I actually got high. I thought I was high, you know, but it wasn't till this particular time that I went to Disneyland. I was at some guy's apartment and I smoked this joint that one of my friends had with him. After about five minutes, I began bobbing my leg up and down and grinning. I continued this enlightening exercise for the better part of an hour, until the guy whose apartment it was came home and threw us all out. I was around eighteen then and had

Al, circa 1964 J.B.D. (Just Before Drugs). PHOTO: AL KOOPER COLLECTION.

been trusted with my parents' car for the evening. Me and my friend hopped in the machine, and I was driving in the direction of his home when my first case of grass paranoia hit. I turned to my friend and asked how I was doing.

"Fine," he said, "but you better drive a little faster. You're only doing five miles an hour."

Somehow I got us both home, but this was definitely the dawn of a new era. Lots of driving around at five miles an hour.

•

After awhile, we convinced ourselves that we'd outgrown Webman's firm and began free-lancing our material. This made things a little more difficult, because instead of a regular salary, we had to sell a song or three every week to survive. This is where I really mastered the art of conning. Our asses were on the fire, and that is the surest way I know to bring any discussion of ethics to a swift conclusion. When desperation overtook us, we'd resort to pre-selling, in a sense, a song we'd written by getting it recorded ourselves. This involved browbeating some weak-willed producer into recording our masterpiece—the function normally reserved for the publisher. What we were doing was actually lessening the publisher's workload by about 75 percent, and it was infinitely easier to convince him to purchase an already-recorded song than some turkey he'd have to go out and hustle.

We'd often have appointments with three different publishers a day. Not having a championship track record to fall back on, we had to rely on sharp wits and a heavy dose of professional sweet talk to open those doors for us. We'd go in and sing our current crop; me like a spinster piano teacher leading her charges through another dreary recital, working our show around to the song that was pre-sold. If they went for it—and you can hardly go wrong by appealing to the laziness in men—we might unload the thing for an on-the-spot offer of three hundred dollars and keep ourselves in burgers for another week. The three hundred was strictly an advance; it was understood we'd receive royalties if the record took off.

About this time, we manufactured a bright little R&B item that none of us figured to be worth all that much. But we managed to sell it for three hundred dollars to my old friend Schroeder, who had developed a very smooth and profitable publishing concern and was interested in signing us to an exclusive writers contract. We'd written this particular song with The Drifters in mind. They were hot, riding a chain of hits telegraphed out to them via the Aldon pipeline (among them "Up on the Roof" and "On Broadway"). They turned the song down, but a West Coast producer named Snuff Garrett, then successfully masterminding Bobby Vee's recordings, picked up on it. By this time we had quit free-lancing and were signed to Schroeder for two bills a week apiece, quite a chunk by our depressed standards. Well, Garrett cut a white version of the tune with Jerry Lewis's thoroughly inoffensive white son Gary and sent us a copy the day it was released.

We were revolted. They'd removed the soul from our R&B classic and made a milkshake out of it. Never mind that who-were-we-to-be talking-about-soul in the first place; this was disgusting. We dismissed "This Diamond Ring" by Gary Lewis and the Playboys on one hearing, and went back to writing songs that might have some chance of selling a few copies.

Suddenly, after a hype-ridden sendoff on the "Ed Sullivan Show" (which was nothing new to us; several of our songs were showcased by Sullivan acts), all you can hear on the radio is our turkey milkshake. Then we're on the charts. 82, 65, 30, 20, 12, 8, 7, 3, 2, 2, and then, after knocking Aldon's "You've Lost That Lovin' Feeling" out of the slot, we've got the *Number One* song in the country. America had finally seen fit to recognize our "talent." We conveniently forgot our previous animosity toward the record and concentrated on basking in as much of the glory as we could squeeze out of the deal. The day the record hit Number 1, we just stared at the charts and laughed and laughed.

We had the biggest song in the country, yes, but we were still broke. Remuneration for a hit record can be a year or more in coming. It's just another music biz irony that you can be at the top of the charts and still be bumming chump change from all your pals. The only course of action is to milk your newfound reputation for dear life; hustle in a bigger ball park.

We drew advances against our forthcoming royalties and affected the trappings of success. Occasional barbershop shaves for that freshly-manicured look; dinner at Lindy's (a high-class restaurant that was a hangout for music-biz successes) for the sake of appearance. And as our milkshake Frankenstein came plummeting down the charts, another Brass-Kooper-Levine special began a hesitating climb up. This one was called "I Must Be Seeing Things," and was courtesy of my old friend Gene Pitney.

Once again, being signed to Schroeder gave us the inside track. Schroeder managed and produced Pitney, owned the record company, and could keep his business perfectly in order by recording songs he already published. But when we were losing at the free-lance game, it was always Pitney who'd take one of our teen traumas and tack it onto an album or make it the flip side of a single, just so's we could eat. When "I Must Be Seeing Things" hit the charts, it felt good to be doing something to repay that kindness.

With two solid chart records, you'd think that all would've been well in the wonderful world of Brass-Kooper-Levine. But alien forces were afoot, and the tide of public taste was pulling out on us. The Beatles were giving Aldon the bum's rush, and an unholy alliance between Bob Dylan and marijuana was fucking with my head in a fierce way. Grass was showing me the same pure visions that it freely dispensed to everyone else at that time, and I found that I could no longer Clearasil-ically compose music. I suddenly saw the inherent dishonesty in what I'd been doing, and prayed to a stack of jazz albums for forgiveness. That's the way grass makes you think, at least at first. It's not until years later that you discover that the crooks and con men had been smoking it all along.

A split was inevitable. The first to go was Brass, who renounced the glory of the music business in favor of a comparatively honest blue-collar job in the Fulton Fish Market, and from then on it was just Kooper-Levine. Our percentages took an instant leap from 33 percent to 50 percent, and that helped dry the tears.

Not long after Brass's exit, one of the producers that we had bombarded with our material took a shine to me and invited me to a session he was producing the next day. The producer was Tom Wilson; the artist he was producing was a guy named Bob Dylan.

Bob Dylan, Mark Spoelstra, Danny Kalb, and Gil Turner. PHOTO: ALICE OCHS.

2

How Does It Feel?

In 1965, being invited to a Bob Dylan session was like getting backstage passes to the fourth day of creation. And, make no mistake about it, a formal invitation was absolutely requisite. There was no just-happening-to-be-in-the-neighborhood of Columbia Studios when Dylan was recording. Sessions for Dylan albums at that time might as well have been strategy meetings for the direction a new alternative culture would take, and it wasn't very often that one of the footsoldiers got the opportunity of watching a five-star general in action.

BE: A little background. Since the early sixties, when vast numbers of people began to shake off the social slumber of the fifties, Bob Dylan had been more than just another writer and singer of popular songs. Elevated by "Blowin' in the Wind" and "The Times They Are A-Changin' " to the status of Great White Social Conscience, he seemed to manufacture his songs with perfect knowledge of the dimensions of the social void they helped to fill. All the loose ends of a possible culture were joined together in the desire to lick his boots; from ban-the-bomb beatniks to college kids who suddenly felt guilty about their soft dormitory existences. And those who couldn't get at Dylan directly—most often because they felt uncomfortable with either his voice or the bluntness of his reality—got to him through other conductors, be they Peter, Paul and Mary or Jack Jones.

Then Dylan turned it all inside out and plugged it into the jet age. Gone was the acoustic guitar and blue jean vision of the street. Gone were the simple songs of social outrage. Gone was the folk hero, and in his place stood a picture of rock 'n' roll gone berserk. For the better part of his previous album, "Bringing It All Back Home," Dylan had employed the use of an electric band, a move that kicked his folk purist following in the teeth. They wanted Dylan only as their narrow minds perceived him and missed the point completely. Dylan wasn't just his songs anymore, he was a life-style. Colorful, amped-up, and crazy; he made sense only if you were willing to unlock your imagination. The session Al describes was for Dylan's first uncompromisingly electric album, the shot Dylan believed would bludgeon the conservative elements of his audience into submission.

I'd been aware of Dylan since the beginning; you could feel his presence in the air. I bought his first two albums because I always made a point of checking out the musical feels around me. I played the records, but nothing happened. I was coming off of a four-year intensive jazz listening binge, and this was too harsh and antimusical to digest in one or two listens. I couldn't hear it.

I was then playing occasional gigs with a neighborhood friend, the not-yet-famous Paul Simon, and his father, a society bass player who'd book all kinds of big band jobs. For the first part of the set we'd sit there with our guitars turned all the way down, strumming along dumbly to "Laura" and "In the Mood." Then every hour we'd leap up and it would be instant Twist-time for fifteen minutes. For being the life of the party, I think we were paid fifty dollars apiece.

One night we played a prom at C. W. Post College with the square band. (You've got to remember that the *kids* were square in those days, too. They still went for big bands rather than rock 'n' roll on those "important" occasions.) While setting up, Paul says, "Man, have you heard 'Baby Let Me Follow You Down' by Bob Dylan?"

Yeah.

"Isn't it fantastic?"

Well, I couldn't dig it, couldn't get next to his voice.

"Fuck his voice, listen to the way he plays guitar. Listen to this," and he began to spew it out note for note on the electric guitar, which made a *big* difference to me.

"Yeah," I said, "I'll have to go back and relisten."

I did, and this time around I enjoyed the records. I also quickly discovered that if I played a Bob Dylan album too loud, it would bring my mother storming into the room in exactly twelve seconds. "Who is that? That's terrible. It sounds like a fingernail on a blackboard. Turn that crap off." His singing definitely struck a discordant note in parents; they were so intimidated by the sound of his voice. That may have even *helped* it all make sense to me.

Little by little the influence crept into my Tin Pan Alley work. "Paper doll princesses" and the like began to show up in our songs, and I made a concerted attempt to convert Irwin Levine. He was into it economically before he dug it emotionally; his cash register brain immediately saw that it would be advantageous to at least take a stab at understanding this weirdness that had infected so many of the people around him. I began fooling around with songs on my own, blatant Dylan rip-offs so totally derivative that they have no redeeming value except as party pieces. I was writing bubble-gum songs by day, working in bar bands by night, and trying to squeeze every possible alternative into the time between. I'd written a song called "Thirty-eight People," a topical little situation comedy about a girl who'd been murdered at a Long Island railroad station while thirty-eight people looked on and did nothing to help her. (Stop me if you've heard this one before.) There was a folk club in Forest Hills, the Cafe Interlude, and I wandered in one Hoot Nite (**BE: An evening set aside by clubs to introduce new talent**, *i.e.*, **anybody with the guts to get up on the stage**) to give them a taste of my new-found relevance.

I wasn't into the scene deeply enough to be anything but a weekend folkie. Like, I had a Goya gut-string guitar; I didn't know that you were supposed to play a steel-stringed guitar. I was a rock 'n' roll guitar player; what did I know from beards and bongos? When I arrived at the club and had to sign in to play, all of the above suddenly occurred to me.

"Shit," I thought to myself, "Al Kooper would never do this. It's almost embarrassing. I'll be—uh—*Al Casey.*"

So I took the stage that evening and performed "Thirty-eight People" as Al Casey.

What I wasn't aware of was that the incident the song describes had taken place right outside the club's window. And that several of those thirty-eight people I was singing about were very probably in my audience, making for a tension that I didn't pick up on until the song was over.

"Hey, man," said an agitated voice from the back of the room, "that bitch was killed right outside this club. Did you know that?"

Stop. "Well, I, err ... thank you very much, ladies and gentlemen. See you next week." Exit Al Casey.

My first appearance hadn't been what you could call a smash, but I stuck with it. The Cafe Interlude became my new hangout, and I quickly assimilated the exotic life-style it presented to me. Within two weeks the Goya went the way of all Goyas, and I had the *right* guitar (Gibson J-200), knew all the *right* names (Woody Guthrie, Ramblin' Jack Elliot, etc.), and even a few of the *right* songs ("Tom Joad," "There But for Fortune," etc.). The people who frequented the club were rigid Pete Seeger types, still hung over from the beat days and maintaining an unabashed contempt for the dishonesty they saw in rock 'n' roll. I wasn't necessarily falling for *that* part of the sales pitch just yet, but I adapted my profile to their attitude as best I could, helped along considerably by their guidance in the finer points of dope smoking. They had sketchy knowledge of my other life, but most likely thought it was just a day gig to keep Al Casey fed.

BE: If they'd known that the guy to whom they were passing the joint was soon to inflict "This Diamond Ring" on the world, they might not have been so charitable.

Through sheer persistence I was eventually offered a weekend gig, three nights opening for somebody named Henry Gibson. I had my folkie set all worked out. A few traditionals, tunes by some contemporary folk writers, Dylan's Dylan songs, and *my* Dylan songs, one of which, "Talking Radio Blues," was an ironically self-righteous put-down of commercial radio, a toothless chomp on the hand that was feeding me. *Doctor Kooper and Mr. Casey.* But nobody came to see us; I guess the weather was bad that weekend or something. Henry who???

About that time, Mike Wallace was putting together a CBS radio documentary on the thirty-eight people incident. He came to the club to tape some interviews and somebody told him about my spiffy topical song, which was then recorded for use as part of the presentation. Figuring this exposure to be an ideal selling point, I started pestering Tom Wilson, Dylan's producer at Columbia Records, with the idea of getting a single of it out as soon as possible. It took five or six visits before I talked my way past his secretary, but when I finally did, he dug it to the extent that we went in and cut the song. He didn't, however, dig it to the extent that the record was ever released.

Still, through this experience Wilson and I became tight. I let him in on the Al Kooper side of me, the Tin Pan Alley songs, some of which he later cut during his tenure at MGM. Our relationship progressed to the point where I could walk past the secretary, straight into his office, which I made a point of doing as often as possible when he wasn't around. I'd sift through his records and cop all the dubs of as-yet-unreleased Dylan material, take them home overnight, and commit them to memory before slipping them back into Tom's pile the next day. These "exclusives" would immediately be incorporated into my Al Casey act and gave it the only bit of charisma it ever had.

Tom had just cut "Subterranean Homesick Blues," Dylan's first electric single, and played it for me prior to its release. *Of course!* On that day, my folkie apprenticeship came to an end. I saw that it was then possible to be Bob Dylan and rock 'n' roll Kooper at the same time, and kissed off Al Casey forever.

•

There was no way in hell that I was going to visit a Bob Dylan session and just sit there like some reporter from *Sing Out!* magazine. I resolved that not only was I going to go to that session, I was going to *play* on it. I stayed up through the night preceding the session, running down all seven of my guitar licks over and over again. Despite my doodling at the piano, I was primarily a guitar player and, having gotten a fair amount of session work under my belt, had developed quite an inflated opinion of my dexterity on said instrument.

The session was called for two o'clock the next afternoon. Taking no chances, I arrived an hour early and well enough ahead of the crowd to establish my cover. I slipped into the studio with my guitar case, unpacked, tuned up, plugged in, and sat there trying my hardest to look like I belonged. The other musicians, all people I knew from other sessions around town, slowly filtered in and gave no indication that anything was amiss. For all they knew, I could have received the same phone call they'd gotten. Tom Wilson hadn't arrived as yet, and he was the only one who could really blow the whistle on my little ego drama. I was prepared to tell him I had misunderstood him and thought he had asked me to play on the session. All bases covered.

Suddenly Dylan exploded through the doorway, and in tow was this bizarre-looking guy carrying a Fender Telecaster guitar *without* a case. Which was weird, because it was the dead of winter and the guitar was all wet from the rain and snow. But he just shuffled over into the corner, wiped it off, plugged in and commenced to play some of the most incredible guitar I'd ever heard. That's all the Seven Lick Kid had to hear; I was in over my head. I anonymously unplugged, packed up, and did my best to look like a reporter from *Sing Out!* magazine.

Tom Wilson made his entrance, too late, thank God, to catch my one act abortion. I asked him who the guitar player was. "Oh, some friend of Dylan's from Chicago, named Mike Bloomfield. I never heard of him but Bloomfield says he can play the tunes, and Dylan says he's the best." That's how I made my introduction to a man who can still make me smile whenever he picks up a guitar.

The band quickly got down to business. They weren't too far into this long song Dylan had written before it was decided that the organ part would be better suited to piano. The sight of an empty seat stirred my ambitions once again; didn't matter that I knew next to nothing about playing a goddamn organ. In a flash I was on Tom Wilson, telling him that I had a great part for the song and *please* (oh God please) could I have a shot at it.

"Hey," he said, "you don't play the organ."

Yeah, I do, and I got a good part, all the while racing my mind in overdrive to find anything that I could play at all.

Already adept at wading through my bullshit, Tom says, "I don't want to embarrass you, Al, I mean . . ." and was then distracted by some other studio obligation. Claiming victory by virtue of not having received a direct "no," I'm off to the organ.

Me and the organ. If the other guy hadn't left the damn thing turned on, my career as an organ player would have ended right there. I figured out as best I could how to bluff my way through while the rest of the band rehearsed one little section of the song. Then Wilson is saying, "Okay, let's try it again, roll the tape," and I'm on my own.

Check this out: There is no music to read. The song is over five minutes long. The band is so loud that I can't even *hear* the organ, and I'm not familiar with the instrument to begin with. But the tape is going, and that is *Bob fucking Dylan* over there singing, so this had better be me sitting here playing *something*. The best I could manage was to play kind of hesitantly by sight, feeling my way through the changes like a little kid fumbling in the dark for a light switch. After six minutes they'd gotten the first complete take of the day down, and all adjourned to the booth to hear it played back.

Thirty seconds into the second verse, Dylan motions towards Tom Wilson. "Turn the organ up," he orders.

"Hey, man," Tom says, "that cat's not an organ player."
Thanks, Tom.

But Dylan isn't buying it. "Hey, now don't tell me who's an organ player and who's not. Just turn the organ up."

He actually liked what he heard!

At the conclusion of the playback, the entire booth applauded the soon-to-be-a-classic "Like a Rolling Stone," and Dylan acknowledged the tribute by turning his back and wandering into the studio for a go at another tune. I sat, still dazed, at my new instrument and filled in a straight chord every now and again. No other songs were gotten that day, but as everyone was filing out Dylan asked for my phone number—which was like Brigitte Bardot asking for the key to your hotel room—and invited me back the next day. I walked out of that studio realizing that I had actually *lived* my fantasy of the night before, but not *exactly* as I had planned it.

•

I was twenty-one at the time of this incident, married to a childhood sweetheart and residing uncomfortably in the comfortable suburb of Forest Hills, Queens. My hair was relatively short, and I wore a shirt and tie because I liked it. I was very confused about what was wrong or right, a condition compounded, I believe, by a great deal of pot-smoking done at this time. Though I wasn't aware of it, my life was changing in ways I wouldn't begin to comprehend until much later. (Like now.)

I returned to the studio the next day with considerably more confidence. My days as a daring organ commando were behind me, and that release of pressure allowed me to get down to figuring out what the hell I was doing sitting at an organ. The other keyboard player was Paul Griffin, who, with a secular black Baptist background, was probably the best studio keyboard cat in all of New York City and certainly the funkiest. I leaned in his direction heavily that day, borrowing a bass line here, a rhythm part there, and generally picked up a lot of basics and the beginning of a style that can be traced directly to his playing. It was the kind of situation where I would have copped from Liberace if he'd been sitting in that seat. (Thanks, Tom Wilson, for not hiring Liberace.)

Recording *Highway 61 Revisited,* Columbia Studios: engineer Roy Halee, producer Tom Wilson, engineer Pete Duria, manager Al Grossman, publisher Artie Mogull, The Great White Wonder, two unidentified people, and Allie listen to a playback. PHOTO: COLUMBIA RECORDS.

Jamming backstage at Newport with Mimi and Dick Farina.
PHOTO: JUDY KOOPER.

Dylan at Newport. PHOTO: ALICE OCHS.

We cut two things that day; "Tombstone Blues" and "Queen Jane Approximately." I was adequate. And elated. That was the last date on Dylan's recording schedule for awhile and ended my contact with him—unless he planned to use the telephone number I'd given him.

•

Eventually the time rolled around for one of the grandest old East Coast traditions, the Newport Folk Festival, and my wife and I made our annual trek north. Despite my pop songwriting and Broadway habits, I had always maintained a healthy affection for this event. Whatever your musical proclivity—even if it was no proclivity at all—Newport was one of the nicest social gatherings you could possibly imagine. Most of the players from New York annually made the pilgrimage, and it was like a Greenwich Village party moved to the seaside. There was a lot of new electric music being played on the barbarian AM radio airwaves that summer, and some of it found its way past the guardians of Newport tradition.

Afternoons were given to slow-paced workshop sessions, which one would browse like a bookstore, doing more socializing than serious reading. On one such late afternoon stroll, I was accosted by Albert Grossman, Dylan's manager.

"Bob's looking for you. Here's some passes; meet us backstage tonight."

And then he was gone. Backstage! I quickly sold the remainder of my tickets and got prepared for my preferred ringside accommodations.

When I arrived backstage that evening, Dylan came running over wearing this top-hat (?) and grabbed me in a bear hug.

"Al Kooper," he said, "how are you? We've been calling you for days. [I had been in Newport.] Good to see you," etc. etc. etc.

What he had in his mind was to put the electric sound of the recording sessions on stage at Newport. "Like a Rolling Stone" was blasting out of every transistor radio smuggled onto the festival grounds, and Dylan wanted to make the penetration blatant. This included my incompetent organ playing, which had suddenly become a publicly recognized trademark of the new Dylan sound.

The group Mike Bloomfield played with, the Paul Butterfield Blues Band, was debuting at the festival that year. So not only was Bloomfield available for duty, Dylan also copped the use of drummer Sam Lay and Jerome Arnold on bass. A friend of Bloomfield's, Barry Goldberg, was "recruited" to play piano (he begged for the chance). The night before the scheduled performance we rehearsed until dawn in one of those huge Newport mansions overlooking the ocean.

BE: Bob Dylan, the king of protest, rehearsing in a millionaire's living room. The times were indeed a-changin'.

Our portion of the show opened with "Maggie's Farm" and concluded with "Like a Rolling Stone." In the middle of "Maggie's Farm," somebody fucked up and Sam Lay turned the beat around, which thoroughly confused everyone until the song mercifully stumbled to its conclusion. But "Like a Rolling Stone" was A-1 and we really got it across. Dylan came off and appeared to be satisfied, and people were yelling for an encore.

If you've read any accounts of that evening, chances are they centered on how Dylan was booed into submission and then returned for a tearful acoustic rendering of "It's All Over Now Baby Blue." A romantic picture, maybe, but that's not the way I saw it. At the close of the set, Peter Yarrow (of Paul and Mary fame and the emcee for the evening) grabbed Dylan as he was coming offstage.

"Hey," he said, "you just can't leave them like that. They want another one."

"But that's all we know," replied Dylan, motioning toward the band.

"Well go back out there with an acoustic guitar," says Yarrow. And he did. That's all there was to it. I was there.

BE: With the influx of rock 'n' roll, the death knell was sounded for the Newport Festivals. Electricity tore the folk tradition to bloody

shreds; its slender wires just weren't strong enough to handle the current. The year that the festival finally ran afoul of local authorities, because of the increasingly rowdy crowds it had begun to attract, the main attraction on the bill was Led Zeppelin.

•

Energized by the Newport reaction, we went back to New York and straight into the studio to finish work on *Highway 61 Revisited*, as the album was to be called. Things went so splendidly that Dylan decided to assemble a full band to accompany him on his upcoming concert tour. I was solid, as was bassist Harvey (Goldstein) Brooks, an old friend whom I'd brought to the sessions.

Bloomfield was a different story. Harvey and I had lunch with him one afternoon.

"You guys going on the road with Dylan?" he asked us.

"Yeah, sure, aren't you?"

"I can't. You guys will be big stars, be on TV and in the movies, have your picture on the cover of *Time*, but I can't do it. I want to stay with Butterfield."

"Why?"

"All I want to do is play the blues, man. Ah likes tuh play de blues."

That was it for Bloomfield. Bobby Gregg, the drummer of the album, also opted to stay home; something about having enough session work to keep him busy.

Mary Martin, a secretary at Grossman's office, took Dylan out to this club in New Jersey to see a journeymen band called The Hawks, who'd done time in their native Canada as Ronnie Hawkins' backing group. Bob apparently liked what he saw that night, because suddenly guitarist Robbie Robertson and drummer Levon Helm were in the picture. This gave us a group (though it did effectively breakup the Hawks). We rehearsed exhaustively every day over a two week period, and the pieces fell together nicely.

•

After rehearsals, I fell into the habit of tagging along at night with Dylan and his left-hand man, Bob Neuwirth, in their regal odysseys around the city. Hanging out in the Kettle of Fish, eating at the Limelight, going to an endless succession of clubs, parties, and recording sessions—with a completely flexible songwriting and session schedule, I had plenty of time to devote to hanging out and soaking it all up. Plus here was a guy who, for no charge, was remaking my entire train of thought. It was like taking a blackboard with all my values written on it, erasing everything, and starting all over again.

Dylan would hold court at a back table at the Kettle of Fish, a seedy little bar on McDougall Street in the Village, that was distinguished only by its musical clientele. Once the place was fairly full they'd lock the doors and Dylan would take over. Word that Dylan was inside circulated in the street, and people would jam up outside the window hoping to catch a glimpse of the action.

Dylan, as always, was buying the drinks. Neuwirth would carry the money, pay the bills, and make all the *necessary* apologies. It was never very long before the room was on a collective drunk (except for yours truly, whose raging ulcer precluded anything stronger than milk). The cast of characters usually included Dylan, Neuwirth, Eric Andersen, Debby Green, Phil Ochs, David Blue, Dave Van Ronk, Ramblin' Jack Elliot, Clarence Hood (who owned the Gaslite, a club next door), myself, and Paul Rothchild (a staff producer at Elektra).

If Dylan got drunk enough, he'd select a target from among the assembled singer/songwriters, and then pick him apart like a cat toying with a wounded mouse—making fun of a person's lyrics, attire, or lack of humor was the gist of his verbal barrage. Dylan was so accomplished at this nasty little game, if he desired, he could push his victim to the brink of fisticuffs. It was all relative to how much alcohol was being consumed by the party of the first part, the party of the second part, or the party in general. When temperatures would threaten to shatter the room's emotional thermometer, it would be good ol' Neuwirth's job to step in and negotiate a temporary treaty over *another* bottle of rum. These nights would usually end with everyone

"Either of you guys know what time the bus stops here?" With Dylan and Doug Sahm. PHOTO: ALICE OCHS.

carrying everyone home and Neuwirth paying a tab that was well into the hundreds.

Dylan maintained a fierce rivalry with his "children" (as *Life* magazine called them), although underlying his antagonism was a comprehensive awareness of their latest albums and career moves. Maybe he wanted to keep everyone on their toes, or perhaps he was just trying to stay awake.

•

After rehearsing for two weeks we were ready to take this *new electric Dylan* on the road. Grossman had booked a couple of impressive dress rehearsals: the Forest Hills, New York, Tennis Stadium for one night; the Hollywood Bowl a week later. The day of the Forest Hills gig, we spent the afternoon doing a sound check and getting acquainted with the big room. It rained in the afternoon, God's little preview of what the night held in store.

This concert took place a brief six weeks after the Newport show, which had been ballooned by the media into a major boo-fest to suit the purposes of the countless articles being written about Dylan "selling out" to crass rock 'n' roll. America was ready for hand-to-hand confrontation with its reckless idol, and Forest Hills would prove to be the battleground.

The concert started off smoothly enough, with Dylan sailing through a well-paced acoustic set to the delight of the overflow crowd. At intermission, Dylan cleared the backstage area and called us into a huddle. "I don't know what it will be like out there. It's going to be *some* kind of carnival, and I want you all to know that up front. So just go out there and keep playing no matter how weird it gets." Yeah, well . . . sure.

Our instruments were pushed into place and we tuned quietly in the darkness. Suddenly an ill-timed wind whipped through the stadium, dropping the temperature at least ten degrees in as many seconds. The crowd stirred at the sound of the tentative drum rolls and guitar tunings, an ominous rumble from the other side of the darkness.

The lights went up and we were into "Tombstone Blues" full force, but the audience was quiet. Too quiet. The wind churned

Soundcheck at Forest Hills: Dylan reeling, Al kneeling. PHOTO: JUDY KOOPER.

around the stadium and blew Dylan's hair this way and that, as if reprimanding him for this electric sacrilege. The conclusion of the song was greeted with the boos all these kids had read so much about and probably felt obliged to deliver. Of course, the barrage was spiced with "Dylan, you scumbag!" "Get off the fucking stage!" and other subtle pleasantries characteristic of our generation.

Dylan didn't flinch. He just bulled his way straight through the hour-plus set. It seemed that even the hero-worshippers were unusually aggressive on this evening. They'd try and claw their way onto the stage to make contact with Dylan, and the police were sparing no tactic to keep them back. One kid was chased behind me by a cop, and as he flew by he hooked his leg on my stool, taking me with him as he went down. I was on my ass and not the least bit pleased about the situation.

Three-quarters of the way through, Dylan stood at the piano to play "Ballad of a Thin Man," a song from the as yet unreleased *Highway 61* album. It had a quiet intro, and the kids persisted in yelling and booing all the way through it. Dylan commanded us to "keep playing the intro over and over again until they shut up!" We played it for a good five minutes—doo do da da, do da de da—over and over until they did, in fact, cool it. A great piece of theater. When they were finally quiet, Dylan sang the lyrics to them: "Something is happening here, but you don't know what it is, do you?" * It was almost as if he'd written the song knowing full well that the moment would come when he'd sing it to this crowd. It was lovely. We then segued into "Like a Rolling Stone," which was number one on the charts that week. Everyone sang along and then booed when it was over!

Dylan pulled his customary vanishing trick, leaving Harvey and me to make our way out into the chilly Forest Hills night unaided. People recognizing our shirts from the stage, reached out to grab us, and believe me, they could have had *anything* in mind. We eventually got out and stopped off at my apartment to shower before driving into New York for the postconcert party at Albert Grossman's apartment in Gramercy Park. Neither of us had the slightest clue as to what Dylan thought of the concert. All we knew was that we played what we were supposed to play, and that the sound had been real good.

BE: A fine pictorial of this concert is available in a section of Dan Kramer's photo book *Bob Dylan*.

We walked into Albert's apartment, and Dylan bounded across the room and hugged both of us. "It was fantastic," he said, "a real carnival and *fantastic.*"

He'd loved it!

* © 1965 Warner Bros. Inc. All Rights Reserved. Used by Permission.

PHOTO: ALICE OCHS.

The following weekend we were scheduled to play the Hollywood Bowl with the same repertoire. Not only had I never been to California, I'd never even seen the inside of an airplane. The band was supposed to make the journey in Grossman's private plane (the Lodestar), but I pleaded to fly commercially for my first flight ever.

I sat between Dylan and Neuwirth coast-to-coast, and they staged the best horror show they could dream up for my benefit. Every time the plane would dip or move the least bit awkwardly, they'd look at each other with blatantly pessimistic frowns and say, "This is the worst flight I've ever been on." Dylan would grip my arm and stammer, "I think this is the big dive, Al." And Neuwirth would cradle his head in his hands and whimper "No, no, no." They'd be ringing for the stewardess every ten minutes, telling her I was very ill and could they please have another airsickness bag? This drama had me ready to pull the emergency latch until I looked around and saw everybody else on the plane calmly enjoying their cocktails and conversation.

While in L.A., me and Harvey shared a room at the Hollywood Sunset Hotel down the hall from Dylan's suite, which was the hub of activity for the week. We got there about two days before the concert, and I went the goggle-eyed hip tourist route all over L.A., which was approaching the zenith of its glory in 1965. I went shopping and saw all the clothes that I'd ever wanted to wear. Incredible brightly colored shirts featuring big polka dots and floral patterns; the kind of mod look that had been imported from London to Los Angeles but hadn't hit New York yet. I immediately blew my entire wad on shirts.

One day a bunch of us were congregating in Dylan's room: Irwin and me, Michael J. Pollard, a few hangers-on, and P. F. Sloan, who was the most blatant West Coast Dylan imitator. Dylan loved having himself surrounded by second-rate mirror images; it was sorta like giving them the Bad Housekeeping Seal of Approval. "Get P. F. Sloan," he'd scream. "Let's have P. F. Sloan up here."

Dylan was in the midst of modeling a new suit he'd just purchased when the phone rang. It was obviously someone Bob didn't want to talk to, because he was trying to hang up almost as soon as he took the call. As he was talking, room service wheeled in an elaborate cart of sandwiches and desserts that Bob had ordered for everyone, and he grabbed a sandwich.

Now at this time it didn't particularly matter whether Dylan was lighting a cigarette, reading a book, or talking on the phone; he was the center of attention at all times. He tried to explain to the guy that he's got to hang up, that they just brought lunch in, but evidently the guy is holding on hard. Dylan nonchalantly takes the egg salad sandwich he's eating and starts grinding it into the mouthpiece of the phone, all the while explaining that it's lunchtime. The guy must have been getting the message, because everyone in the background was loudly in stitches. Dylan's parting shot was to pour his glass of milk into the phone as well, saying, "Well, so long, thanks for having lunch with us." Totally oblivious to the milk and mayonnaise all over his new suit, he just strolled into the other room to take a nap. End of audience.

•

The Hollywood Bowl concert was a sharp contrast to the Forest Hills show, in that it defined the essential differences between the hipness of the two coasts. The audience (and what an *audience:* Gregory Peck, Johnny Cash, Dean Martin, the Byrds, Tuesday Weld, and others) listened attentively to the new Dylan and, after polite initial applause, got caught up in the electric feeling. Soon we were getting thunderous ovations. In the middle of the encore, my ulcer began to go haywire. I didn't have my pills with me, so the most logical plan of action was to try and latch on to the coattails of Dylan's escape at the end of the song. This part of the evening was as well planned as any military maneuver, so it was just a matter of timing.

I didn't know what the plan was, but I figured that if I followed Dylan, I couldn't go wrong. Boy, that little fucker could run. By the time he was halfway down the back ramp, the car, driven by his old friend Victor Mamudes, was already moving. "Wait for me, wait for me," I yelled, as they pulled Dylan into the car.

They yanked me inside barely in time. We were doing about ten miles an hour already, and when the door closed behind me Victor quickly accelerated. Due to the tremendous amount of sweat Dylan and I contributed by our presence, all of the windows in the car fogged. When I glanced up, the speedometer said eighty-five and a girl was screaming, "You're going the wrong way! We're headed for a brick wall! Turn around, Victor!"

She was perfectly correct, and Victor executed a turn that would have given Evel Kneivel an ulcer to rival my own. Out of the Bowl we wheeled, making it to the hotel before the audience's demands for more had died away. I took a double dose of pills and crashed.

•

As no other concerts were scheduled, Irwin and I stayed on in Hollywood for an additional week. We were theoretically there to hustle our songs, but mostly we just let L.A. hustle us. I had gotten into weird, almost Eastern, guitar tunings, a curiosity I discovered I shared with David Crosby. I resolved to do some public experimentation along these lines, and the ensuing course of events proved to be yet another Kooper scam.

Irwin and I showed up at a club called the Troubadour one Monday evening, where we met up with a guy named Dick Webster, who played all manner of off-the-wall drums and percussion instruments. It was Hoot Nite, and the three of us took the stage as the "Sacred Cow." I sat cross-legged on the stage, fucking around intently with my weird tunings on an acoustic guitar. Webster banged away on his many percussion devices. And Irwin, who has a somewhat Asian face to begin with, put on sunglasses and dressed like an Indian. We made up three songs on the spot, Irwin singing absolute gibberish while the rest of us did our best to match his level of ludicrousness. The

The view from behind the piano, Hollywood Bowl soundcheck: Dylan and Robbie Robertson. PHOTO: AL KOOPER.

Two refugees from a hat store: Harvey Brooks and Al Grossman.
PHOTO: AL KOOPER.

audience, thinking some great cultural event was taking place, accorded our sham respectful applause. We didn't get any record contract offers, just a whole lot of laffs.

•

When I finally made my way back to New York, Dylan's office dropped the full itinerary for a major tour in my lap. Noting that the tour stopped in Texas, I began to give serious consideration to making my exit from this traveling circus. I mean, look at what they did to J.F.K. down there, and he was the leading symbol of the *establishment*. So what was going to happen when Bob Dylan, the most radical vision of the counterculture, paid them a visit? I wasn't sure I wanted to find out. This was actually good timing for me, because I was about to get canned anyway. It seems that the remaining members of the Hawks were eager for the gig, not having been at all happy with their separation from Levon and Robbie.

One morning I called Dylan and asked him what he was doing.

"Eating a piece of toast and listening to Smokey Robinson," he replied.

"I'm going to have to leave the band," I said.

"Okay," he said.

"See ya," I said.

"Okay," he said.

PHOTO: MGM/VERVE

3

Kooper Sessions

The release of *Highway 61 Revisited* elevated me to the position of a session player in demand. People I'd never heard of were calling and offering me jobs, talking to me as if we'd been friends since childhood.

I'd get a call and they'd say, "Can you make it at 8:00 P.M. at Bell Sound Studios?" And I'd say, yeah, I'm free, who is it for? I had no money to speak of, so I should have jumped on *any* opportunity that came my way. But I just couldn't see sitting in some studio for four hours, being forced to play music that I found distasteful. I'd tell them up front how really inexperienced I was, that I didn't sight read music (I did, but not well enough to make any claims for myself) and then ask if they were still interested. Without fail they were.

I remember getting a call once for a session that I had absolutely no desire to do. The only way I'll do this, I told the guy, is if you pay me double scale.

BE: Double scale meant twice the union fee paid a musician for a session, and only the heavy players like King Curtis could command so exorbitant a remuneration.

This was just a joke; my way of expressing my unwillingness to play the date. So imagine my shock when he says, "Okay, double scale," without even stopping to think about it. It was a wonderful ego boost, but ludicrous all the same.

They didn't want *me*, of course, they wanted the new "Dylan sound." When "Like a Rolling Stone" hit number one, all the Mister Joneses might not have known what was happening, but they sure knew what to *do* about it: *Cover it! Copy it! Get in there and grab a piece of the action for yourself!* The tip-off was when I'd tell them that my guitar playing was actually superior to my elementary grasp of the organ. "Oh no," they'd say. "We want you to play keyboards." They'd have a place pencilled in for me, usually right in the spot where you'd find the organ runs on a Dylan record. Clever.

It was embarrassing. When I got to the studio, I'd be treated a little too nicely for comfort. There I was, surrounded by some of the finest players in New York City—Gary Chester, Everett Barksdale, Eric Gale, Frank Owens, all of them people that I'd once dreamed about getting the chance to play with—and I was getting preferential treatment while they were treated like hired help. I mean, these were *exceptional* musicians; they had ears, they knew I wasn't hotshit. I was still new to the instrument; I practiced constantly and was getting better, but I still wasn't much more than adequate. It just happened that my simplistic style of playing fit the groove of Dylan's new approach. Taken out of context, it could be funny. Or worse.

For kicks, I'd go out and buy all the records that aped the Dylan sound. I'd take them over to Dylan's house, and we'd play them and laugh. The imitation Kooper organ was always the star attraction. I had a "style" based on ignorance. And then to hear these great musicians imitating my inexperience! Really.

When they hired Kooper, though, they got everything *but* the Dylan sound. I wasn't about to give them the easy carbon copy they were looking for; that would have been pure prostitution. (Not that I hadn't whored in my Tin Pan Alley days, but my moral fiber was becoming thicker.) Without Dylan, these guys would never have been calling me, so why put his trip on sale for chump change? I just went to those sessions and played what I thought the songs required. Take it or leave it.

In *certain* respects, my presence *did* add color to any session I was on. At this time I was trying desperately to grow long hair, and I was wearing the bizarre clothes I'd picked up on my West Coast trip. I wore a gold earring in my left ear (nonpierced) just for good measure. All this was to affirm my mental departure from the old Al, and wardrobe weirdness has been a trademark of the new Al ever since. Okay, now that we've dressed the baby, let's set him loose in the playground.

•

I received a call one day from Al Grossman's partner, John Court, to do a session for the Simon Sisters, they being Carly and her sister Lucy, in an early performing incarnation. I arrived at the session and walked smack into Gary McFarland, who was the arranger on the date. Then, as I glanced around, I recognized nearly half of Count Basie's band sitting there waiting to play. *Oh no. How was I gonna get through this one?*

I looked at the keyboard parts and, sure enough, they were far beyond my reading capabilities. So I walked over to McFarland and did an instant confessional.

"Look, Gary, I'm a huge fan of yours and just about everybody in this room. But I can't read the part you wrote for me, and I'm feeling real sick about all this, and who do I have to fuck to get *out* of this movie?"

He was tremendously reassuring. He told me to sit on the part and play what I felt like playing; that that was why they'd hired me in the first place. I sat down at the organ and sweated through the run-throughs. But, by sessions's end, I'd played decently and had certainly not sabotaged the entire day as I had fantasized. Once I got through *that* session, the others were a relative cinch.

•

Sometimes session work could be great fun; a prime example were the sessions for Tom Rush's *Take a Little Walk with Me* album. What was happening musically at the time was an incredible cross-pollination effected by Dylan (folk) playing electric (rock). Former folk acts were playing the old rock 'n' roll songs of the fifties and considering them folk music. Chuck Berry was playing the folk festival circuit along with Muddy Waters and Jimmy Reed. Old R&B was now the darling of the folk set. Rock was slowly taking over as the primary contemporary musical expression by simply incorporating everything in its path. Explosive as this takeover was, the development still caught most of the record company A and R men (artists and repertoire—an early synonym for producers) with their backgrounds down.

At Elektra Records, Jac Holzman had fashioned a fortress of folk music on the talent of artists like Tom Rush, Judy Collins, and Phil Ochs. Marc Abramson and Paul Rothchild were Holzman's producers in residence, but they were spiritually unprepared to handle the new electric music. This is not to belittle their talent, which was proven immense (Rothchild, for example, later went on to produce all the big hits of The Doors); merely to point out that their talent had never been channeled in this direction.

Tom Rush, however, had been performing stuff like Bo Diddely's "Who Do You Love" and the Coasters' "Shoppin' For Clothes," and was anxious to make a rock/folk album that would mirror his affection for this music. Marc Abramson called and asked me to put a band together for the project, and I readily assembled a tasty little unit composed of Bruce Langhorne on guitar, Harvey Brooks on bass, Bobby Gregg on drums, and yours truly on lead electric guitar (playing all the tunes I'd played, when they were new, with the Royal Teens) and keyboards. We went into the studio and just rocked our asses off, having one hell of a time and getting paid for it to boot. *Take a Little Walk with Me* was one of the most enjoyable recording experiences I've ever had.

BE: And, in its own way, one of the more influential albums of the period. Rush was on the board of directors of the folkie establishment, and his seconding of Dylan's electric motion carried a lot of weight.

There were so many sessions that my memory banks are too overloaded to recall them all. Once I played behind the daughter of the owner of one of the largest department store chains (which sold *a lot* of records) on the East Coast. Must have been her birthday, so Daddy bought her a recording session with the best musicians in New York. The only reason that I even remember this is that every couple of years she turns up on a different label, usually around the same time of the year.

I was in on the first session at the new Columbia Studios, for Bruce Murdoch. I played on a Judy Collins version of Bob Dylan's "I'll Keep It with Mine," for which Bloomfield was expressly flown in from Chicago. I cut a Spider John Koerner session produced by Felix Pappalardi. An electric version of "I Ain't Marchin' Anymore" with Phil Ochs. David Blue's "Stranger in a Strange Land" for Jim and Jean, another Tom Wilson production. I did sessions with Peter, Paul and Mary and the Butterfield Blues Band; just sessions every day for months and months all through 1965.

Much of the above session work was for Elektra, and they returned the favor by asking me to participate as an artist on an album they were compiling called *What's Shakin'*.

BE: That album, released by Elektra in 1965, was a sampler record showcasing the Butterfield Blues Band, The Lovin' Spoonful, Eric Clapton and the Powerhouse with Stevie "Anglo" Winwood and Jack Bruce, and of course, Al. It's an essential for anyone interested in midsixties rock 'n' roll; well worth the search required to uncover a copy these days.

They asked for two tracks, I cut four, they used one: "I Can't Keep from Crying Sometimes," a Blind Willie Johnson tune I adapted and arranged. I played both piano and overdubbed guitar, with the asistance of two young New York musicians soon to figure prominently in my past, drummer Roy Blumenfeld and bassist Andy Kulberg. The recorded quality of the track seems almost garage-level in retrospect, but there's a certain unselfconsciousness about it that the several subsequent versions, by myself and others, doesn't approach.

BE: The information booklet in the *What's Shakin'* package identified Al as a "New York legend." Nat Hentoff, in his review of the album, commented that "Kooper may be a New York legend, but certainly not for his singing and piano playing," a statement which holds true to this day and remains among Al's favorites.

Tom Wilson rang me up one day and requested my services on yet another session. I always gave Tom top priority because of the tremendous debt I owed him, and said sure. I arrived for this date in my typical out-there fashion, earring and all, and was introduced to a roomful of my contemporaries known as The Blues Project.

PHOTO: ALICE OCHS

4
Life with the Jewish Beatles

Up to this time, *The Blues Project* had been Elektra record number EKL-726, "a compendium of the very best on the urban blues scene." Which was a nicer way of saying "this record contains the performances of twelve middle-class 'white punks on dope,' who have for the most part successfully achieved the ambience of twelve 'black bluesmen on booze.' " I had no idea that there was a *band* walking around with the same name and identical values. One of the performers on that album, a guitarist named Danny Kalb, had appropriated the name (with Elektra's blessing) and with the assistance of four friends, had assembled a New York Jews for Electric Blues crusade.

To wit: Danny Kalb was an established singer-sideman on the New York blues scene, having gained his measure of prominence from appearances on recordings by Dave Van Ronk, Judy Collins, and the aforementioned *Blues Project* album. Danny's love of blues was shared by Roy Blumenfeld, a neighbor of his from Mount Vernon, New York. When no one sensitive enough to play drums could be found in the Village, Roy taught himself to play and joined the group.

Steve Katz, who appeared on a similar Elektra white blues album, *The Even Dozen Jug Band*, (which also treated us to the talents of Maria Muldaur, John Sebastian, and Stefan Grossman) and was, like Danny, a student of Dave Van Ronk, signed on as second guitarist. Andy Kulberg, a classically trained flautist from

Buffalo, New York, whose professional experience had been limited to a few polka bands in his hometown area, was overjoyed at the prospect of being able to leave his heritage behind and become the group's bass player. Tommy Flanders, a refugee from the Cambridge, Massachusetts, rock 'n' roll circuit, was designated the group's Mick Jagger in an effort to increase its commercial potential.

When I walked in, this session was just one more entry in my appointment book, but for these chumps the experience was probably terrifying. It was not only their audition session for Columbia Records, but also the first time that some of them had been inside a recording studio. I was surprised to find that they'd chosen an Eric Andersen song, "Violets of Dawn," to hang their futures on, as this was not your standard bluesband selection. But as I soon discovered, this was not your standard bluesband.

The two guitarists were fingerpicking a weaving construction of the chord sequence, and I made the mistake of attempting to weave with them on the piano for the better part of an hour. I kept trimming my part until there was almost nothing there, but what little was left seemed to do right by the arrangement. All this time I had no idea whether what I was doing was even vaguely what they were looking for, which was making me more than a little paranoid. But we finally got a good take and everyone was smiles. When the session ended they invited me to lunch the next day. Feeling relieved, I accepted.

At the appointed time I met Danny, Andy, and their manager, Jeff Chase, at the Keneret Restaurant in the Village, and we sat down for a pleasant little lunch. I assumed that they wanted to hire my hands for the rest of the album, and that the purpose of the lunch was to fatten me up so they could jew me down. All of a sudden they were asking me to *join* the band, which caught me so completely off guard that the best initial response I could muster was a "huh???" It took me about thirty seconds to sort out all the pros and cons: the Dylan trip was definitely over, the studio work was getting a little samey, and here was a chance to practice and improve on my instrument, and maybe even make a couple of bucks.

Danny Kalb. PHOTO: MGM/VERVE.

Eric Andersen. PHOTO: ALICE OCHS.

Andy Kulberg. PHOTO: ALICE OCHS.

Roy Blumenfeld. PHOTO: ALICE OCHS.

"Sure. I'll do it." That was the beginning of a three year whirlwind.

This whirlwind, however, had modest origins. First of all, I had to be initiated into de Mystic Knights o' de Blooze. BB King, Muddy Waters, Son House, Blind Willie Johnson; these were names I'd seen but music I'd never heard. Danny would play me these treasures for hours on the guitar and the phonograph until he was satisfied that the sound had been strummed into my head permanently. But it was a loving assimilation, because the music appealed to me emotionally as well as intellectually. While I was growing up with R&B and gospel music, somehow traditional blues had escaped me. In New York, R&B and gospel music were readily available on the radio, but it required some fancy dial twisting to scare up a Muddy Waters record.

Then, of course, there were the rehearsals. When no one will hire you, you can't do anything *but* rehearse. Unless you could play the entire Top Forty or you had a hit single out, club work was nonexistent. Plus, we had no matching suits or other related all-American paraphenalia. This is not to say that there weren't a few $39.95 tuxes from the Royal Teen days in *my* closet right next to the skeletons. Everyone else in the band was far more advanced in the area of rejection of middle-class values, while I was still living in Forest Hills and taking in at least two hundred dollars a week from sessions and royalties. But I respected their dedication, and longed to make that move myself.

To get back on the track, our first rehearsal took place at somebody named Julie's apartment on Grove Street in the Village. I still couldn't tell Steve and Andy apart—all I could see were noses and work shirts—but I knew Roy was the tall one and Tommy was the one with the Rolling Stones haircut. Kalb and Flanders ran the band and that was fine. Tommy the singer would tell Danny the guitarist how he wanted his backgrounds painted, and Danny would assign the proper brushes and strokes.

We rehearsed about four hours, 'til the neighbors called the cops. It actually was not very intelligent to have set up a rock band in the living room of a cramped Village brownstone, but what did we know? *We were crusaders!* Rehearsal space was at a premium due to the simple fact that it cost *money*. (The Lovin' Spoonful were rehearsing in the foul basement of the ever-popular Albert Hotel at this same time and for the same reason.)

Somehow, we managed to scrape together enough cash to rent space in 1697 B'way and move the crusade uptown for awhile. The Tokens and other people I knew in that building would come down to see what ol' Allie was up to, but it wasn't the kind of music that paid the rent, so of course none of them understood or were the slightest bit impressed. But the juxtaposition of images involved in the Blues Project rehearsing at 1697 was like a symbolic farewell to a set of values that no longer applied. I knew which side *I* was on.

By this time, I was *hooked* on the blues crusade. I began to really understand the cultural potential of the band, and how important it was that kids find out about Muddy, BB, and the whole blues scene in general. They had probably OD'd on Bobbies Vinton and Vee, and I came to see what a positive alternative blues was.

We were *not* a traditional blues band in the sense that Paul Butterfield's group was. They played the tunes almost exactly the way the original records were, like a Top Forty blues band. We'd change *all* the arrangements, never doing a tune like someone else had done it. This is not to say that we didn't do other people's songs; we just did 'em our way. We also did folkrockier things than Butterfield's scope allowed for, like Donovan's "Catch the Wind" and Bob Lind's "Cheryl's Goin' Home."

Meanwhile Butterfield was out there proselytizing and making his contribution to the crusade; and as long as we're owning up, he was probably responsible for *starting* it. His band had built a strong following in their native Midwest area, and a much-acclaimed first album on Elektra, along with Al Grossman's high-powered management, was causing a ripple of interest to swell into a wave. The three B's—Butterfield on harp and vocals, Mike Bloomfield and Elvin Bishop on guitars—created a powerful three-pronged attack, aided and abetted by an unflagging rhythm section comprised of Sam Lay on drums,

Tommy Flanders. PHOTO: ALICE OCHS.

Steve Katz. PHOTO: ALICE OCHS.

Jerome Arnold on bass, and the later addition of Mark Naftalin (his pop was the mayor of Minnesota—I can't spell Minnie Apolis) on keyboards. They were a kick-ass group, and it was dangerous for any lesser band to share the stage with them.

Not long after I joined up, Tom Wilson left Columbia for MGM-Verve. Columbia waived their claim on us, so we moved with him and signed with Verve-Folkways, MGM's answer to Elektra. It was also around this time that our manager was able to secure for us a week's berth at a Village jazz joint called the Cafe Au GoGo. This club had gained fame for hosting the likes of Stan Getz and Lenny Bruce (actually what it gained was *infamy*—the owner, Howard Solomon, was brought to trial on Bruce-induced obscenity charges but was later vindicated) and being the location of Stan's popular *Getz Au GoGo* live album. I don't think they had ever played a rock band (that's us) before, but business stank and Solomon was desperate. God knows, he must've been! To put it diplomatically, we were green. Our hair was somewhere between short and growing long, nobody but me "dressed" to go onstage and, most of all, we were still learning. Hardly headliner material. Hardly even support band material.

Then a funny thing happened. After we played the week, he hired us for three more. I don't think it had anything to do with the business we did (there wasn't any); he was probably just fascinated because he was so unaccustomed to seeing acts survive. We'd take each night's proceeds and adjourn to the bar across Bleeker Street called the Dugout. In an hour we'd be as broke as we'd been earlier that evening, but too drunk to care.

The ironic part was that all through the early stages of the band's career, I waived taking a salary, due to my outside income. And, because of my ulcer, when the take was squandered on alcohol I didn't get to participate on *either* level. (Another illustration of the band's poverty was that Tommy would show up at your house, ask to use the bathroom, and then tie it up for an hour by taking a shower.)

As the three weeks wore on, a few brave faces reappeared.

The Birdman of Bayside. PHOTO: ALICE OCHS.

Fans! They helped us gain a little confidence, and I think, experience aside, that's what we *really* needed.

Tom Wilson and Verve, meanwhile, were trying to figure out how to record (or relate to) us. They didn't know whether we were Paul Revere and the Raiders or The Mothers of Invention. Neither did we, really. Based on our embryonic popularity, Howard Solomon was planning a Thanksgiving holiday all-blues show to feature some of the more accessible blues greats. Looking to subsidize his advertising campaign (that means get somebody/anybody else to pay for it), he turned to Jerry Schoenbaum, then president of Verve-Folkways.

The original concept Solomon had envisioned was to get some money to promote this potential Thanksgiving turkey starring his house band, The Blues Project. Schoenbaum took it five steps further by getting Verve to underwrite the *entire* week in exchange for the recording rights. Because the majority of the artists were either signed to Verve or unsigned to any label, this was a way of assuring at least three or four albums to amortize the initial investment.

"The Blues Bag," as it was so trendily baptized, was advertised extensively both over and underground for Thanksgiving week of 1965, featuring Muddy Waters, Big Joe Williams, Otis Spann, John Lee Hooker, and the band of white Jewish kids who taught them everything they knew, The Blues Project. Prior to this cannibalistic undertaking (record company eats black singers—defecates them on black vinyl), nobody had been adventurous enough to bankroll a blues package in a small club on the white side of the tracks. Solomon & Schoenbaum (attorneys at law?), however, found themselves with sold-out, standing-room-only performances for the entire week. And twenty minutes after Muddy Waters had brought each capacity house to its feet, The Blues Project would take the stage.

I think they picked us to close the show strictly by virtue of the fact that we were unquestionably louder than anyone else on the bill. It was almost embarrassing, our black heroes having to warm up for us; I guess that's just the American way. Nonethe-

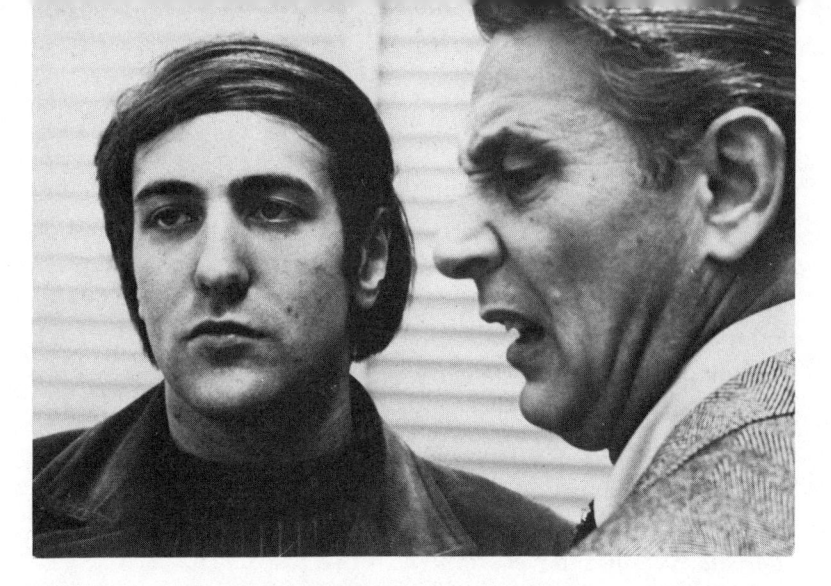

Jerry Schoenbaum, president of Verve-Folkways, giving Danny an unnecessary tongue-lashing.

less, here was our first substantial captive audience. And the weird thing was that it was 95 percent white, while the show was 95 percent black.

These days it's not unusual for BB King to play a sold-out show with nary a black face in the audience, but in 1965 it was quite a novelty. We looked out into a sea of faces that we had all seen in the next room in the college dorm, ahead of us at the draft board and sitting behind us in temple. These kids were just younger versions of us, and not *much* younger at that. And they knew it—we were theirs! We didn't have the cool assurance of a Muddy Waters, the natural instincts of a John Lee Hooker, or the sheer talent of an Otis Spann, but now we had an inkling of what *they* felt like when they faced a packed house at the Apollo or the Regal.

BE: The Apollo and the Regal were theaters in New York and Chicago respectively that catered exclusively to R&B. Their prestige came not because they were beautiful facilities—they were only one notch higher than dumps—but because the crowds that frequented them were the most demanding that an R&B artist would ever perform in front of. They knew their music, and if you were anything less than top of your form, they'd make their displeasure known swiftly.

We came out fightin', trying to stay alive and get our point across any way we could. It wasn't like we sat down at a conference table one day and said, "OK, Danny is gonna jump up and down and make all these faces, and Al is gonna wear a cape and a taxi-driver's hat, and Steve, you get a Beatle haircut, and Tommy you do splits while we're playing solos." We were real in our own way, McLuhan's media children flexing their newly acquired muscles. We may have borrowed our music, but our demeanor was something new.

In the face of all the talent and roots that surrounded us, *we stole the fucking show every night!* In retrospect, it's easy to see why. It was our audience's equivalent of when we sat in dark theaters watching the knife fight and the chickie-run in *Rebel Without a Cause*. We sat in those seats and we *squirmed;* relating even though we weren't always able to duplicate.

When we left the stage, the audience was sweating as heavily as we were and was probably as exhausted. We got 'em with Energy and Volume; and in those days E + V = $$$. The whole time Verve's tape machine was rolling, getting our first album down. Robert Shelton, the music critic for the staid *New York Times*, applauded our efforts in print, and when the Blues Bag reached its delirious finale, it was only natural we should resume residence at the GoGo and fill the joint ourselves.

It was a small fame we had achieved, but it put spending money in Howard Solomon's pocket. The band, of course, was still starving, because we maintained the same overhead, and the money hadn't improved dramatically enough to affect our paychecks. And we had our problems. We needed new equipment; so it was decided that we'd pool each weekend's take for that purpose, leaving the rest of the gross for rent and food.

Tommy didn't go for it. He felt that he was a separate case in that he was the singer and we were the band. He paid for and looked after *his* axe (the throat) and would we please pay for *our* instruments 'cause he didn't know how to play 'em, so why should he be party to buying 'em? Also, Tommy didn't happen to be born Jewish, and that was the *only* thing the rest of us had in common.

Our first gig: Tommy, Danny, Steve, Roy, Andy, and Mr. Polka Dots. PHOTO: AL KOOPER COLLECTION.

Whatever the reasons, there was a showdown, and Tommy, bless his heart, stood his ground. The man had the courage of his convictions, and I respect that. It cost him his gig, though, and it shook us bad, 'cause a lot of charisma walked out the door when he did.

•

Tommy's departure automatically consigned Steve and me to singing chores, whereas previously only Danny had shared Flanders' field. I picked a Chuck Berry tune, "I Wanna Be Your Driver." Steve took over a song he'd written that Tommy had been singing, called, strangely enough, "Steve's Song." I took a gospel song I knew and rearranged it for Jewish bluesband, and that's how we started doing "Wake Me Shake Me." One night, Roy broke a bass drum pedal in the middle of a show, and Steve pulled out Donovan's Top Forty folker "Catch the Wind" and did it percussionless, and we kept that in the show. Little by little we fashioned a new repertoire. Danny, however, remained the chief lead singer and band leader.

Soon after, Jeff Chase signed us up to the William Morris Agency (ta-da!). An international booking office saw potential in, of all things, us! We cautiously stepped outside the confines of the Cafe Au GoGo to test our stuff in other situations. Our first out-of-town gig was as opening act for Stan Getz in the gorgeous vacation retreat of Pittsburgh, circa dead of winter. We had no cars, trucks, or roadies (guys who schlep your equipment), and certainly no money to rent any of the above. So we self-schlepped all our amps and equipment down to Grand Central Station and hopped the train.

Boy, it was surreal. Dirty hippie kids lugging all these guitars and crap onto a train populated primarily by old ladies and sailors on shoreleave. And of course the train was delayed and we got there real late; Stan Getz had already gone on and was pissed-off that he'd had to. The audience was there for one reason only: Stan Getz. It was actually quite considerate of them to wait a few minutes after he'd finished while we set up. Halfway through the first number, however, they unanimously

"No, we do not play church socials!" Manager Jeff Chase, taking care of business. PHOTO: ALICE OCHS.

agreed it was *too loud* (not enough rockers, too many jazzers) and most of them left. We played with all the gusto a train ride to Pittsboig can inspire, and, mercifully, it was over. Once again, we packed up our stuff, headed for the train station, and caught the late Flyer to New Yawk. God, it was depressing. No reward, no relief, no standing ovations, no encores. Just old ladies and sailors.

Our next "road trip" was different: we had *two gigs* booked. World tour time! The first was a Friday night at Swarthmore College, and then Saturday night at Antioch College. This time we tried it with two cars and one roadie, the band in one car and the roadie and all the equipment in another.

Swarthmore's a neat little school tucked somewhere out of my memory in rural Pennsylvania, and it was holding its first Annual Rock 'n' Roll Festival (yay!), so we knew that *volume* would not be a problem. Swarthmore was probably the breast at which rock journalism suckled. It was here that the first rock mag of fairly intelligent criticism was born. A mimeographed two-sheeter completely authored by student (not the singer) Paul Williams made its way around the campus and eventually found its way to press. This was a good two years before *Rolling Stone* introduced its first issue.

Anyway, we pulled into Swarthmore and the students welcomed us with open arms. We were surprised; they actually knew who we were! We availed ourselves of their dorm showers after our grueling drive and hit the stage only ten minutes late. It was no contest. The Energy-plus-Volume Machine trampled 'em and, two encores later, we piled into the cars and began our long trek toward the hinterlands of Ohio and our next victim.

In the car, exhilaration. We had carried our sound out of New York, made it portable, and it had worked on 'em outatown. Our enthusiasm soon gave way to tedium as we plowed toward our destination. We drove all night and it seemed that we hadn't even put the slightest dent in our mileage. We drove all the next day as well, but by sunset we were still hours from Antioch. Finally, at who knew what time, we staggered into Yellow Springs (that's what we felt like), Ohio, and pulled up in front of the auditorium.

Talk about cuckoo. No sleep, lots of drugs, and a few of our old ladies (allowed to come along for the ride out of inexperience) pissing and moaning all the way. It was two hours after we were supposed to have played; but were they uptight? *No way.* They were just glad we were *there*. The auditorium was jammed with people who wanted to, as they say, "boogie." We made it to the now-familiar dorm showers and mounted the stage on by-then shaky legs.

Antioch is one of a handful of "progressive" institutions that was totally into psychedelics at the time. The entire first two rows were watching us thru kaleidoscopes! No one in the band felt much like being awake, much less playing, but there wasn't even time to vomit. Due to the epic proportions of our journey, we did *not* play well. But did they give a shit? Could they even tell the difference? Not two, not four, but *five* encores! I couldn't believe after each one that we were going up there again.

This was one of the major weirdnesses of being on the road. Sometimes you could play the best music you'd ever played, and they'd just sit there on their hands; no encore, no nothin'. And then, as on this particular occasion, you shovel an hour's worth of dinosaur shit on 'em and get standing ovations and twenty encores. This usually helped to temper your respect for the people you played for.

They put us all up at the school and we slept like rocks for the first time in two days. Sunday afternoon everyone woke up refreshed and the plan was to fly back to New York; fuck this stupid driving shit! Monday night, however, I was committed to be in Nashville to play on some Dylan sessions (for the album *Blond on Blonde);* so I decided to stay over at the school one more night and fly directly to Nashville. I tagged along while some school kids drove the whole entourage to the airport, bid my wife goodbye, gave the boys five, "see ya in a week," and copped a ride back to the school with these two chicks.

They were the first "dedicated fans" of the Blues Project (it being too early to call them groupies). I never made it to the school. I just barely made the plane the next day. It is taxiing towards the runway and it's snowing like in *Dr. Zhivago.* The plane, all of a sudden, stops and this tiny jeep pulls up carrying yours truly, looking a little worse for the previous night's shenanigans. They drop the ladder down and I, unaware that the flight had originated in New York, board the plane only to be greeted by much laughter and fingers pointed in my direction. The other passengers were all music business people that I knew from New York: Al Gallico, the publisher, Bob Morgan, the producer, and Bobby Vinton, the Polish person. And they can't understand what I'm doing in a jeep on the runway during a snowstorm in Columbus, Ohio, at nine o'clock in the morning. And I ain't tellin' either. I believe in the magic of rock 'n' roll!

•

Verve was wavering about releasing our album. Tommy was so much a part of the live recordings they felt it would misrepresent the band to release the album in its present form. It was hurriedly decided to return to the GoGo and record some additional material with Steve and me singing lead. Back to the beginning, almost. We booked a week *during the afternoons* (the nights unfortunately were taken already) and announced on the radio that we were recording live, and lots of kids came for free after school. It was weird gettin' it on at three o'clock in the afternoon, playing a whole set, then going outside where it was still light out.

Anyway, we got what we needed, and shortly thereafter our first baby, *The Blues Project Live at the Cafe Au GoGo*, was delivered in record stores all over America. Although, in retrospect, the sound quality is not unlike playing a shirt cardboard on your turntable, it *more* than served its purpose. For one thing, it was the first rock album to appear on the charts without benefit of the requisite "hit single." This made the industry look up and take notice.

At the same time, adventurous FM stations (based on the successes of WOR in New York and KMPX in San Francisco) were switching their normally staid formats to progressive rock programming. Many kiddies were rushing out to buy new radios so they could be "with it." The FM stations took us to their hearts and played our album vociferously at a time when the AM stations completely ignored us. The record actually sold. I remember the company's first ad, which was placed in all the trade publications (*Cashbox, Billboard,* etc.). The headline read: "This Album Has Already Sold 22,000 Copies. That's 18,000 More Than The Street Thought It Would!" What they failed to tell you in the ad was that it was also 19,000 more than Verve thought it would.

MGM-Verve began to show some confidence in the band.

Rockin' out at the GoGo, 1966: Andy, Steve, Danny, Roy, Al.
PHOTO: CHUCK STEWART, MGM/VERVE.

They flew us to L.A. to appear at their annual sales convention. The high point of that trip was when five starving hippies and one starving manager—us—invaded Trader Vic's restaurant and ran up a two-hundred-dollar dinner tab and charged it to MGM with a belch and a satiated smile. Our appearance at the convention was well received, and the record company pencil-pushers got a glimmer of the potential in what we were doing. We made our L.A. debut at the Troubadour, but no one showed up to notice. Fucking snobs!

While we were in L.A., we also went into the studio to work on our next album. Jack Nitszche, who wrote arrangements for Phil Spector and the Stones, came down to produce us, but we were so into it that I'm afraid we ignored him (fucking snobs!), and he left the studio throwing his hands up in the air in frustration.

Billy James, a friend of mine from the Dylan days and also head of public relations for Columbia Records West Coast, helped us cut a few tracks, but for political reasons was credited as Marcus James, his eight-year-old son. (Probably the youngest producer in record biz history.) We cut a song I'd written called "Fly Away," and a Chuck Berry tune, "You Can't Catch Me." Then we hit the road. Or actually it seems that the road hit us.

•

We took our by-then long hair and ridiculous clothes out into Middle Amerika and she bitterly retaliated:

In Cedar Rapids we were hissed and booed as we deplaned.
In Boston some guy tried to run me over as I crossed the street.
In Canada they threw whiskey bottles at us as we left the stage.
In Maryland we were refused lodging in two hotels.
In Detroit we were refused service at an airport coffee shop.

Not being into martial arts, we retreated to the sanctuary of drugs. I mean, we tried to keep ourselves as incoherent as possible at all times so we wouldn't realize what indignities we were being put through. It was real lonely. I realize that you're probably slapping your head and saying what a fucking cliché! Wait a second. Let me explain.

It's 1966 and we play in your small college-town gym. Everyone brings a date to the show and consequently there are no "singles," if you catch my drift, left over. You've arrived in the afternoon to your Holiday, Days, or Ramada Inn room, where the staff lets you know that you are most assuredly *not* welcome. You rush out to a soundcheck, where a skeleton college crew is totally unprepared for you, and the simplest matters wind up taking hours. You've got maybe enough time to return to the hotel and shower (lunch, dinner, forget it—they wouldn't serve you in the restaurant even if you *had* the time to eat) and then race back to the gym. Then it's wait around while the first act goes on late, and plays twice as long as it's supposed to, and makes the audience real irritable just in time for you to go on.

Your big hour. Now that was *golden*. It was, for sure, the only enjoyment in the entire schedule. God forbid you played a *lousy* show; then suicide seemed like the only alternative to the boredom, frustration, and futility. After a quick perusal of the premises for a smiling female (nope!) it's back to the hotel where the kitchen is (you guessed it) closed and it's 11:30 and all you can pick up is on the TV; waving flags and priests.

So practically all of us got high a lot. I'm surprised we weren't junkies. It's probably a miracle of sorts that no one in the band inclined that way, but mostly we smoked hash, grass, and opium, and took some occasional mescaline. Imagine being revered on stage for that golden hour and then being rushed back to your hotel cell. You felt like some talented animal in a zoo on temporary leave. It made us closer to each other, 'cause we were all in the same boat. If deep down we hadn't really dug each other, we could never have pulled it off (we did that a lot, too).

•

With our record out and on the charts, our modest level of fame spread out of the general Eastern area and across the Great Divide. The agency booked us heavily and we went out and got 'em all. Sometimes for convenience we would charter small aircraft (five to eight seaters); Buddy Holly Specials, I called 'em.

The first pilot to fly us in a charter was Stanley Pell, the brother of famous west coast arranger Dave Pell. He owned a

STOL (Short Take Off & Landing) Aero-Commander Number 68 Romeo that sat six plus pilot and co-pilot. We had an afternoon appearance at a college in Waterville, New York, and an evening's engagement at Steve Paul's Scene Club in New York City. William Morris suggested we rent a plane and turned us on to Stanley, who flew Dionne Warwick and some of their other clients.

Everyone was a little uptight as we clambered aboard that first day, but Stanley had an excellent planeside manner and, placing Danny in the co-pilot's seat (he was the most nervous and Stan figured if he could *see* everything was OK, he'd be cool), he taxied down the runway and took off—directly into a huge blizzard. The plane bounced around the sky like some crazed pinball, but it's different somehow when you can see the pilot, hear the radio transmissions, and see out the front window. There's no element of doubt, no matter how bouncy the ride. Suddenly, Stanley pointed off to the right side and announced we was in de area. "There's the runway," he said, and we all looked down.

It looked like a teenie black magic-marker line on a huge sheet of fluffy white paper. He swung around and headed straight for it. The plane was swaying from side to side but he was dead on it and he landed smoothly to a standing ovation (well, half-standing). We never thought twice (well, maybe once) about flying with him again.

Sometimes we'd take turns sitting in the co-pilot's seat, and he would let us take the wheel and steer the plane. I had it once and was supposed to maintain an altitude of 7,000 feet. I held the wheel steady as a rock for 45 seconds until Stanley nudged me. "You better bring it up a little, Al, you've just dropped 1,500 feet." It's a good thing he never passed out or anything. That wheel is so fucking sensitive, I can't believe that shit about Karen Black flying no 747!

Once we had a gig in Canada and we couldn't get Pell. It was the opening of Expo in Montreal, and we were playing in this huge indoor coliseum that held close to 100,000 people. Every-

Hotel room dungeon time: Steve, Al, Danny, Roy. PHOTO: ALICE OCHS.

thing converged on this boxing ring (!) in the center of the room that they used for a stage. You'd think they'd erect a little stage or something for the fucking fair. No way. So it was with great trepidation that we stepped through the ropes and addressed this mostly French-speaking, short-haired audience.

It took us about five seconds into the first song to realize that the "sound system" for our concert was also the same one that the announcer would utilize to say, "And in this corner . . ." We looked at each other, somehow made it through one more instrumental (singing was impossible in a room that size with a tinhorn PA system) and then departed rather ungracefully through the ropes in the general direction of the dressing rooms, dodging a hail of bottles as we went.

Andy went to the bathroom and didn't return. Our roadie rescued him from a slicing at the hands of a couple of young punks. The climax of all this bad feeling was a short but genuine fistfight between Steve and me. Both our nerves were short and shot, and somebody said something dumb to somebody and that was it; flailing arms everywhere.

Like I said, we were with a new pilot this trip. The pilot, it seems, had inhaled a few drinks at the gig (which is against the law) but no one got on his case. He still had to fly us home, after all, and nobody wants an *angry* drunk pilot, do they?

We get back on the plane real shaken. He taxies to the runway; so far so good. Fingers crossed. He revs up the engines for takeoff and then this haughty voice comes over the intercom: "Fasten your seat belts, kiddies, it's time to cheat death once again!"

Danny was especially terrified during this two-hour jaunt and, as we thankfully began our descent over New York, he began howling in pain. It seems that his ears were bothered by the pressure drop, an affliction that can sometimes befall anyone who flies, and he was in terrible pain. We made three separate descent attempts courtesy of our polluted pilot. Finally, with mostly green faces and Danny locked in Roy's arms howling away, we feathered down to terra firma, grateful to be alive. For the most part, however, flying was a commonplace thing to us, and I never thought too much about it. It was like getting on a subway or a bus to go to work in the morning.

Limousines also found their way into our lives at this time. We got a big kick out of the incongruity of it all; chauffered Cadillacs picking us up at our slumboxes in the Village. Danny's place was the most urban, to put it politely, of all our abodes, and it was real cute picking him up on Welfare Avenue while he glanced nervously from side to side to make sure no one saw. It was embarrassing to get caught by our contemporaries in the limo, 'cause it was contrary to our image (De Blues Project Gets Down Wit Da Street Peoples, Right On). But if anybody stared in the windows at us, they'd find five third-fingers raised skyward for their trouble. The Blues Project salute.

•

I remember the destruction of one of the last bastions of our collective sanity; the crack that caused the dam to burst. It was the day that Steve, who wore his hair combed straight back, came to rehearsal with a genuine Beatle haircut. God, we gave him so much shit, but at the same time we were proud of him. He had sacrificed his previous image (which wasn't shit, anyway) on a scissored cross of rock 'n' roll. Actually, it was his mother who cut his hair. With this one great transformation to her credit, and the fact that she came cheap, Mrs. Katz became the official Blues Project barber. There were no hip barbers or haircutting establishments in those days; even in the Village you took your chances.

Steve lived at home but he was unusually tight with his parents; so tight that he even used to bring chicks home after gigs. I couldn't relate to it. I mean, you schlep a chick all the way to the suburbs so she can go to bed with this rock star, and next morning she wakes up to the mother making pancakes and the father pulling out the family album. If I was a chick, I couldn't have handled it. But Steve made out OK, so what the fuck do I know?

Andy lived with his wife, Phyllis, in a tidy little apartment on

Perry Street. Danny, as I implied before, lived in a place that would give *any* parent nightmares. For a kitchen he had a two-warmer hotplate. That was it, no refrigerator or even a sink. After visiting his apartment once, I never questioned Danny's right to sing the blues. Roy lived on the Lower East Side in a little pop-art cubbyhole where he collected fabrics and presidential seals. I think I was only there once; we used to room together on the road, but off it Roy kept pretty much to himself. I lived in a six-flight walk-up, midtown on Lexington Avenue at Thirty-fifth Street. I was separated from my wife and living with a girl who was soon to become the next in my procession of marital mishaps.

Everyone was a heavy pothead by now except Danny. In 1965, I'd had a Thanksgiving party at my house, and Danny got loaded with us and we loved it. He confessed to us that the only other time he'd gotten high was during the Cuban Missile Crisis, because he thought we all were gonna go and he wanted a headstart on heaven. But I was high *all* the time. Before I went to sleep I'd stash a joint under my pillow so I could get loaded before my feet touched the ground in the morning (which they seldom did).

And of course we were influenced by the sensibility of the Beatles as in *A Hard Days Night*. *Our* movie, which was never realized, had some fabulous footage in it. I'll recount to you some scenes from our true-life screenplay.

In mid-1966 there was this huge one-night blues festival at Stonybrook University on Long Island, We were the headliners. This is where *The Blues Project Live At Town Hall* was recorded, but Town Hall sounds much better than Stonybrook University, so don't tell anyone, and I won't either.

Anyhow, it was an important night to us. We went out there early in the afternoon to check the recording balances and make sure everything was A-OK. It took all day, and we finished just as they let the people in to get their seats. The lineup was Chuck Berry, Muddy Waters, Richie Havens, John Lee Hooker, Dave Van Ronk, David Blue, and us.

Steve's previous image. PHOTO: MGM/VERVE.

    While the rest of the band watched the show, I escaped with a newly acquired woman in search of a place to get better acquainted. We ended up consummating our mutual feelings for each other on the indoor handball court. Just as we are concluding the swoon, our roadie busts in. "Al! Where the fuck have you been! Everyone's looking for you—" glancing at his watch—"Holy fuck! You got forty-five seconds before we're announced!"

    Well, you know the bit where you're running and putting your clothes on at the same time. I mean no time for a fond

The Nose and the Neck: Andy and Al. PHOTO: AL KOOPER COLLECTION.

farewell or a kiss goodbye. I make it backstage just as they're announcing the band. In full gallop I bound onstage half-dressed. Danny's already into the intro to our opener, "Goin' Down Louisiana" *(I had been Goin' Down Linda myself)*. I've got my pants and a white tee shirt on, that's it. No sox, no shoes. (Usually, I took the opportunity of appearing onstage to indulge my taste in bizarre costumes. There were kids who'd come to see us just to laugh at my clothes.) So when the spotlight hits me for my solo and the band sees me for the first time in a fucking tee shirt with a huge hickey on my neck (which I of course can't see) they can barely keep playing, they're laughing so hard. It was wonderful.

The time came to complete our second album and get it out as soon as possible. Pressure again. It was always rush time when we were supposed to record. In those days ('66) the artists did not have nearly (or any of) the control they do today. They had no say in what studio was used, had no concept of the stereo mixing processes, and were seldom consulted regarding the cover art. Sometimes (as with the Byrds on "Mr. Tambourine Man") they didn't even play on their own records. They just played and prayed, and that's the way it was with us as well. At least we got to play on our records (maybe that's what our problem was).

    We used to get the spare time the Animals weren't using. They'd call us the day before and say, "OK, tomorrow from one to six you're at Regent Studios and we need to get three tracks cut." Tom Wilson would be there. Since he produced both us and the Animals, I'm sure he didn't know who was gonna walk through that door at one o'clock; he just sat there and ground 'em out. They'd set us up and we'd play our little hearts out. Three takes a tune was all we were allowed, due to time restrictions. But we didn't know any better. I was always amazed when I heard other records that were so precise; I thought everyone made records the way we did.

    One day we were recording "Two Trains Running," which was ten minutes long and one of our live cornerstones. There were many tempo changes and subtleties in it. We were halfway through it and no one could even see anyone else 'cause they've got all these partitions and isolation screens up, yet we were playing it better than we ever had. Danny is singing it live and doing an incredible job and I was creaming. We got to a real quiet spot in the song and suddenly Danny's saying, "Stop the tape. Hold it. I can't go on!"

    We put down our instruments and looked at each other. I could see in everyone's eyes that, yes, *everyone* thought it was the best we'd ever played it. *Not* Danny. I guess the isolation and the fact that he was having trouble hearing his guitar and keeping it in tune threw him. So we took a break for awhile and then started from the beginning again. And we lost that whole take. Nowadays, they would keep it and have us start where it broke down, finish it and splice it all together; we could've been heroes and you would never know. So we're playing it again and all of a sudden magic happens. We got to the same spot, a place where the band just stops cold for four beats. One of Danny's strings slipped a half-tone out of tune, and he used that space to play a riff incorporating the necessary tuning back up of the string. Clever. We all kept going and finished the take. When we played it back, the *one lick* was so incredible that it warranted keeping *that* take for the album. Listen for it.

Two of my new songs, the first I ever wrote all by myself A.D. (after drugs), were included on the new album. "Fly Away" is a transition song; like a lyrical bridge between my two marriages. The other was "The Flute Thing," the song that changed Andy's life. Andy was primarily a flautist, but aside from a lick here or there, he had no vehicle to showcase his skill in that area.

One night in Cambridge, Massachusetts, on the floor of Jill Henderson's apartment, while Danny was cooking beef stroganoff for everyone (God, what a stickler for detail that Kooper is!), I composed a little instrumental on Danny's acoustic guitar. It was based on a cadenza played by Kenny Burrell at the conclusion of some jazz tune.

In those days, Andy carried his flute everywhere. Not that he would play it all the time, but it was his last link with the classical world, and I guess he needed some reassurance. Well, out it came and he quickly digested this bit of pap I had dashed off (it was so easy a child with an ocarina could've joined in).

Soon we were rolling all over Jill's apartment with our new song. Two days later we were playing it on stage with extended solos by everyone except poor Steve, who had to learn to play the bass in order to free Andy for flute. Later on Andy, frustrated at not being able to be heard over our OV (oppressive volume), surprised the fuck out of us by matter-of-factly drilling a *hole* in his precious flute and installing an *electric* pickup. There was no looking back now; the Buffalo Philharmonic would not have stood for any of *this* tomfoolery. Andy, along with Steve's slicked-back hair, had joined in the rock 'n' roll crucifixion.

Danny gets into "Two Trains Running." PHOTO: MGM/VERVE.

The electrification of the flute was added, unfortunately, *after* we'd hastily recorded "Flute Thing." However this was just the beginning for Andy, who appears to be, chronologically, the first electric flautist of note. Not satisfied with that distinction, he concocted a complex and expensive set of pedals and effects for his instrument, which he was always primping and improving in his spare time. It used to sound incredible (he incorporated time delay, fuzz tone, wa-wa, and echo effects), but it pissed the rest of us off because we ended up spending more money on that one damn thing than for anything else on stage. Not to be outdone, I started collecting weird percussion instruments (Pakistani bells and toy pianos, styrofoam blocks, and Indian clappers) and integrating them into the freer sections of the song just to bust Andy's balls.

Recently, I had the opportunity to visit with Gregg Allman, and in a discussion of old times, it came out that he had been a staunch Blues Project fan.

"The thing I remember most about your old band," he recalled, "was the Kooperfone."

Gregg was making reference to an instrument also known as the Tubon (pronounced Tube-on) or ondioline (pronounced ondio-leen), the precursor of today's electronic synthesizers. My boyhood chum, Eric Krackow, first turned me on to the ondioline when we were both about seventeen. It was the invention of one Jean Jacques Perry, a Frenchman who was deeply involved in electronic music and its live reproduction around the same time as Robert Moog, who built and designed the synthesizer that bears his name.

BE: Perry recorded an interesting but little-known album for Vanguard Records called *The In Sound—From Way Out*, one of the first pop-electronic albums.

Perry brought two of his prototypes to New York from Paris and gave public lectures and demonstrations to turn people on to this new instrument. He leased the two instruments to Carroll

The Pied Piper of Newport: Steve, Andy, Roy, Danny. PHOTO: ALICE OCHS.

Music Company, an instrument rental house, and they in turn allowed musicians to rent them for recording sessions. Eric Krackow's Aunt Doris worked at Carroll Music, and mentioned it to Eric one day, and he, in turn, passed the information on to me. Dick Hyman, a New York studio player, and I were the only two people I knew taking an *avid* interest in this new toy. The very first time I used it was on a Gene Pitney session where we were doing one of my songs, "Don't Take Candy from a Stranger." This predates the Blues Project by two years. Dick Hyman and I each played one on the session as sort of a horn section effect.

Later, Guild Instrument Company imported a condensed version of the ondioline, called a Tubon, from Sweden. This was sent over by a friend of ours (Mark Dronge, Mr. Guild's son) for my perusal. It was love at first sight. Due to its curious design, it was entirely adaptable to our live show. It was a cylindrically shaped affair with a keyboard cut into one side and volume and tone controls set in the other. You would strap it on and hold it like a saxophone. It only played one note at a time (the highest note depressed), and I developed a technique of playing with the heel of my hand as opposed to using individual fingers on the keyboard.

I'd listen to John Coltrane records (the Tubon at its best was capable of imitating the range and nasal quality of Coltrane's instrument, the soprano saxophone) and transcribe his scales and solos and convert them to my heel-of-the hand playing technique. It was so off-the-wall that, combined with every other musician's lack of interest in it, the band dubbed the instrument the Kooperfone, a name that stuck. It was heard for the first time on "I Can't Keep from Crying," another track from our new album. (I also suspect that it appears on Del Shannon's "Runaway" and the beginning of "Baby You're a Rich Man" by the Beatles.)

Projections, as that album was titled, was released in mid-1966. Its initial sales surge was almost three times that of our first album. We were movin' on up. This time out I'd written four of the nine songs on the album and was becoming more than just that "piano player in the corner," as I'd initially envisioned myself. Ambition can be like a cancer, starting slowly, then working its way through you. I was being consumed by an inner drive to do more and more.

This, of course, caused tremendous conflict in the band. The group, once entirely Kalbesque, was now up for grabs. And it was knock-down and drag-out. Danny was, is, and always will be a traditional bluesman. I was, am, and always will be a rock 'n' roller. It was a battle between the purist and the bastardizer.

I used to carry around a cane "for effect" until one day, in an argument, I realized I was capable of crowning Danny with it and had to throw it away. But I don't wish to mislead you. It was all of us. We had nothing in common spiritually, and maybe that's why the band was so strident and energy-filled. It certainly didn't do much for our mutual communication. But, as I mentioned before, somewhere down there was this deep love we had for each other. Years later, it brought us back together one more time, to do a reunion concert and album.

Once, in an effort to bring all the suppressed animosities to the surface, we all sat down in a psychiatrist's office and had what was probably the first rock-group therapy session. The doctor was known to all of us, as we had all seen him on solo visits. God, it was like an emotional Fourth of July. Everybody got their deep-seated likes and dislikes out, and the air was charged with discontent. When it was over, we all walked out and just stared at each other. Right then and there we decided that one more session would probably get us a lot tighter as people, but would definitely end the life of the Blues Project. That was the finale of group therapy.

•

It was around this time that we made a big shift in management. We had outgrown Jeff Chase, who was basically just Danny and Roy's high school buddy. It wasn't that we thought he was dishonest, simply that we had graduated to a plateau where more acute business manipulation was required. Poor Danny drew the shortest straw and had to break his old friend the news, a task he was not real fond of. Jeff was not real fond of our decision, either, and ran to the attorneys. We ended up making a $20,000 settlement with him, to be doled out over the years. This eventually buried us financially and kept us from pulling ourselves up to a comfortable level. Nowadays, twenty thousand is a piss in the ocean, but nowadays he probably would've settled for $150,000.

At any rate, we went manager shopping and, let me tell you, I'd rather comparison shop for diarrhea. All these guys spreading their wily wares out on their desks and enticing you with their version of whatever they assume your fantasies are. And of course the guys you really want to manage you are invariably the ones who could give a fuck less whether they ever see you again. After a month of eeny-meeny-miny-mo, the burden of our future success fell into the soft hands of one-time concert promoter Sid Bernstein.

Sid, who was a serio-jolly fellow and claimed to believe in the blues crusade, also managed The Rascals, who were doing quite well at the time. Our performing price soon doubled, but our salaries remained the same due to Jeff's management settlement and our increased overhead. In retrospect, I figure that getting any richer might've corrupted the music, so maybe it was just as well.

•

We were out there playing, too. We played at the San Francisco State College Folk Festival with Richard and Mimi Farina, Mark Spoelstra, and Malvina Reynolds. We drew quite a few people to the Newport Folk Festival of 1966, too. That was a weird gig for me. Just prior to my departure for Newport, I was feeling particularly awful and went to the doctor.

"Doctor! Mr. MD! Tell me what the fuck is wrong with me?"

He took some tests and said, "Son, you got mononucleosis. I heartily recommend that you enter the hospital."

We were playing at The Scene in New York until the Newport gig, and right after that we were booked into an important new New York disco called the Phone Booth. I made a deal with the doc to take lots of medication, rest as much as possible, and not to kiss anyone above the waist, and as soon as the Phone Booth gig was over, I'd indeed enter the hospital. (They'd probably carry me in.)

All through Newport, of course, I'm running a fever and having to keep a low profile. Miraculously, I made it through reasonably intact. The night we opened at the Phone Booth, the band had installed an army cot outside the dressing room. It was a good thing they did, 'cause toward the end of the first show I passed out cold.

BE: Don't think for a second that Al was, or had any notions of

Spreadin' the word in San Francisco: Steve, Andy, Danny, Roy, Al. PHOTO: ALICE OCHS.

being, any kind of a martyr. The Blues Crusade could've functioned just as well with one less organ player, as Al himself would certainly tell you. But it was a question of economics. The cancellation of a Blues Project date might mean that Roy's rent or Danny's grocery bills wouldn't get paid.

I was rushed to the hospital and was glad to be there. Paul Harris, a friend from Queens who had been the recipient of all my studio work when the Project became too time-consuming, was called in to replace me at the Phone Booth on two hours' notice. He fit right in and saved the gig.

Due to our insecurities about not having a charismatic-type lead singer, we hired on a young girl named Emmaretta Marx, who could sing quite well. Emmaretta was not Jewish, but she *was* black. She would bound onto the stage halfway through the show and liven things up a bit. She also brought along her own "roadie," a Jean Shrimpton-ish mod delight named Gail. This meant we had to carry *two* extra people and pay higher hotel bills, so Emmaretta was definitely *on trial*.

Gail caused a little friction in the band, 'cause everyone fell in love with her at the same time and didn't bother to tell the others (or Gail, for that matter) about it. A few indecent proposals from a bunch of emotional cripples sent Gail fleeing straight into the arms of Frank Zappa, where she remains Mrs. Zappa to this day, mother to Moon Unit, Dweezle, and others. Emmaretta turned out to be a passing Project pick and, after missing more rehearsals than she could afford to, was returned to from whence she came.

We were packaged on Blues Shows quite often, and ended up becoming friendly with those performers whom we had once revered from a distance. Muddy Waters, BB King, James Cotton, Otis Spann, and Howling Wolf became close friends to us. Usually, if we played on the bill more than one time with these people, they would drift into the dressing room to find out what we were.

All except Chuck Berry. Early in our careers, we backed up

Vogue's worst-dressed couple of the year: Gail and Al. PHOTO: ALICE OCHS.

Frank Zappa announces his betrothal to Gail. PHOTO: ALICE OCHS.

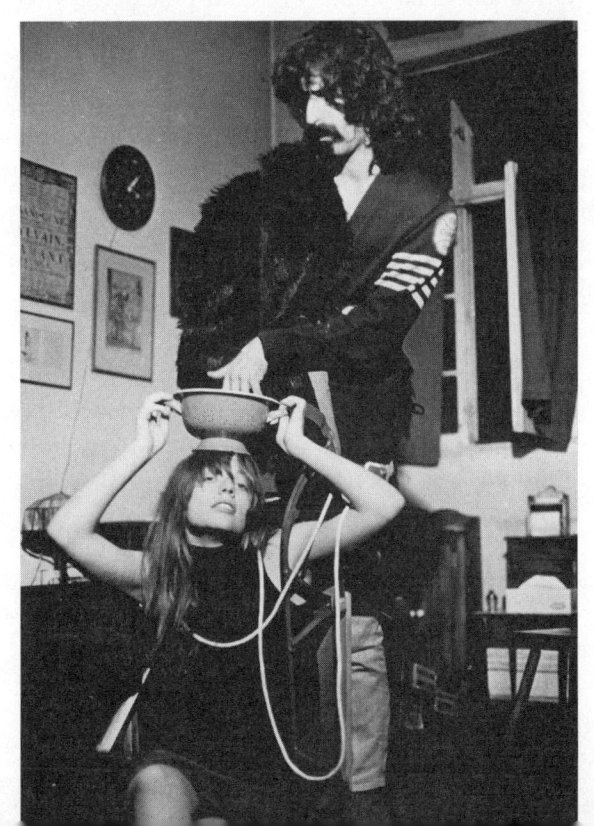

Chuck Berry at his first New York solo concert. He was a scary guy and a tough leader, and *never* did he encourage any friendship. He was strictly professional: "All you do is watch my foot. When it go up in the air, get ready. When it hit the ground, if you playin', stop. If you ain't, *start!*"

When we were in town, we hung out mostly on Bleeker Street. A few of us would make the journey uptown to Steve Paul's Scene, but that was mainly for whoring. Usually, it was the GoGo, the Dugout, or the GoGo's competition across the street, the Bitter End. But for laying back, about two blocks west on Bleeker was Alice Ochs' apartment.

Alice was Phil Ochs' ex-wife, and she lived with a girlfriend in a cozy pad that overlooked all of Bleeker. Every folkie and folkrocker hung out there and Alice would sit in the corner with her Nikon and snap away as 1965, '66, and '67 rolled by. We used to get a few extra bucks from Verve and take Alice on the road with us so she could keep on takin' all those pictures, many of which enhance the text herein.

While in San Francisco, we played at the first concert thrown by a hippie cartel known as the Family Dogg. They had rented out a huge ballroom on Sutter Street called the Avalon and booked three rock groups for Friday, Saturday, and Sunday nites. We headlined over two local bands, the Sons of Adam and the Great Society (which at the time contained the husband and wife talents of Darby and Grace Slick). It was April 12, 1966, and the weekends that followed gave local rockers an alternative to Bill Graham's shows at the original Fillmore. Eventually, they went the way of all hippie business ventures, and Graham resumed his stranglehold on rock in Frisco.

•

By now, we were at our peak. We were New York's most beloved underground band, the toast of Cleveland, Ohio, the "enfants terrible" of Cambridge, Massachusetts, and invaders from Mars to the rest of the country. We would often need good security to guarantee trouble-free exits from concert appearances.

My favorite memories from this time period are locked into a ten-day stage show we did for a local jock in New York over the Easter vacation in March 1967. Murray The K's Easter Rock Extravaganza featured the Blues Project, Cream, Wilson Pickett, The Who, Jim & Jean, The Chicago Loop, Mitch Ryder, The Mandala, The Hardly Worthit Players, and the Jackie The K (Murray's wifey) Dancers. It was the American debut for The Who, Cream, and the Canadian Gospel-rock group Mandala, all relatively unknown commodities here, and it was convenient and inexpensive for Murray to fit them into the framework of this fifties-style rock 'n' roll revue.

I had played many trips like this with the Royal Teens. You play your one, two, or three hits and get off quick. Five shows a day, shuffle, shuffle, etc. Ludicrous, huh? *You bet.* Murray tried to media it up by shooting film on each of the acts and running the clips during set changes. But in order to make a profit, he had to keep the time of each show down, so many of these trailers hit the cutting room floor. A nice idea, though.

We shared a dressing room with Cream and got friendlier with them than with anyone else in the show. It was their first U.S. trip, and diving directly into this show must have given them a more than distorted look at life in America.

The show took place at the now-defunct (an oft-used phrase in this here book) RKO Fifty-eighth Street Theater. On Easter Sunday, in between shows, Jack Bruce, Steve Katz, and I strolled over to Central Park, where New York's First Annual Be-In was taking place. It was the counterculture's free Easter party, and we thought we'd have a looksee. Everyone in the area was attired in glorious flower-power finery; chicks were passing out wine, candy, popcorn, cakes, and dope. As I stuffed a few handfuls of popcorn into my mouth, it occurred to me that perhaps some folks might've combined the dope into the food (San Francisco style), and maybe discretion was in order in any acceptance of free handouts. I mentioned this to Steve and Jack, but they hadn't eaten anything.

On the walk back to the theater, I discovered I had shut the

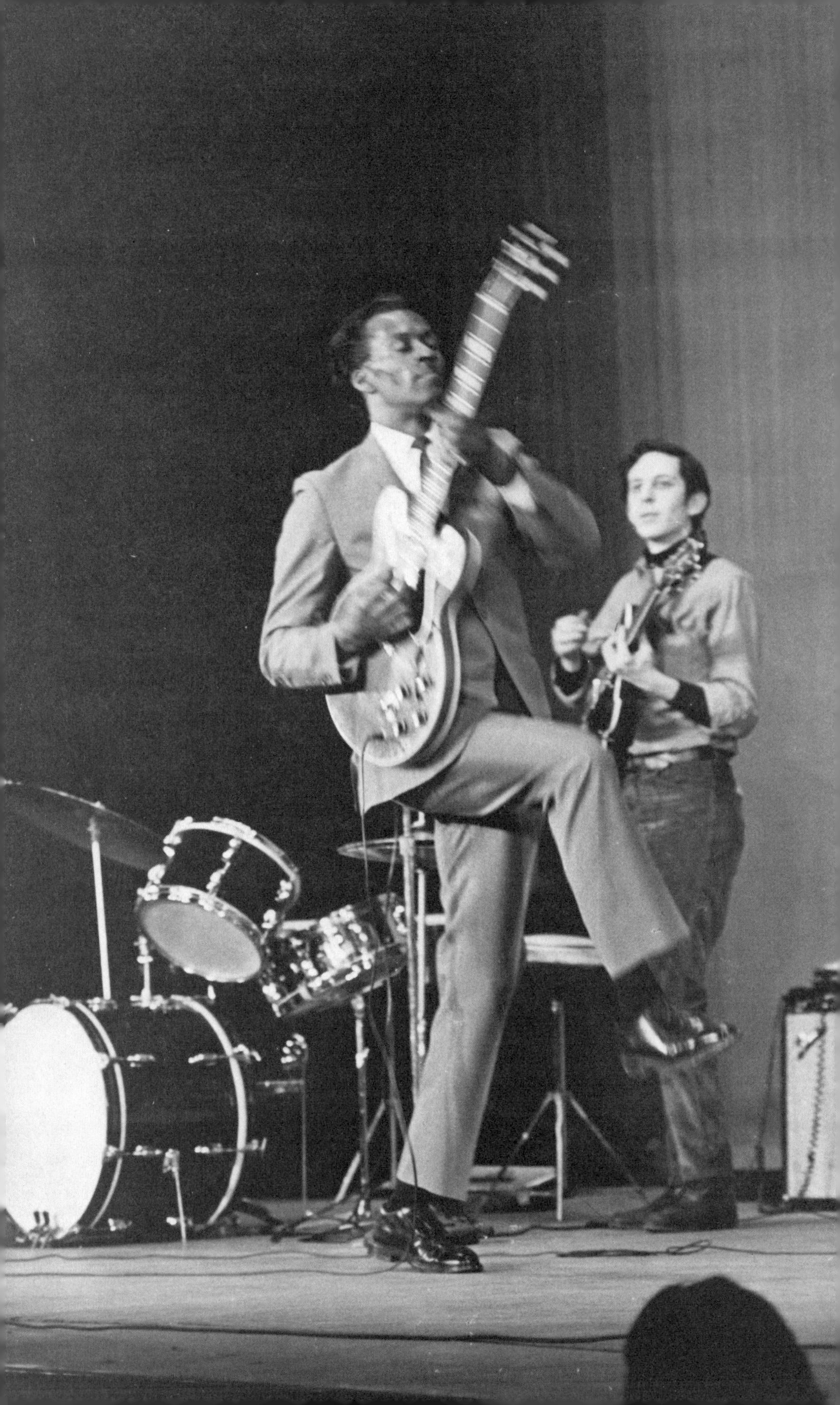

Posing with local Frisco rock group SFPD and their equipment van: Danny, Steve, Emmaretta, Andy, Roy, Al. PHOTO: ALICE OCHS.

Steve forgetting to watch Chuck Berry's foot. PHOTO: ALICE OCHS.

barndoor after the horse was loose. Boy, was I gooned out. It's hard to pinpoint what I was experiencing, but I do remember it was positive all the way. The band wisely decided to play the next show without me. Our roadie took me out into the audience and, for the first time in my life, I watched the Blues Project play. A pleasant trip.

Cream was having a time of it. For a band that later became known as the stretch-out group of all time, fifteen minutes to do three tunes was a bit restrictive. They did "I Feel Free," "Spoonful," and alternated closing with "Traintime" or "Crossroads." It was uninspired compared to the shows they would later whip on people. (*Wheels of Fire* is playing in the background as I'm typing this, and I'm grinning.)

The Who were another story. I had read all about them in the imported English papers, so I knew what their trip was. I'd seen pictures in *Rave* and *Disc,* and was looking forward to seeing firsthand their guitar-smashing climax. They were chosen to close the show, and wisely so. The first day everyone in the cast stood in the wings to see what all the talk was about.

Well, they launched into "My Generation" and you could feel it coming. Keith Moon flailed away on these clear plastic drums, and it seemed like he had about twenty of 'em. It was the first time any of us colonists had seen the typical English drumkit. There are usually six to eight tom toms of various sizes as compared to two or three in most American drumsets. And huge double bass drums, one of which said *THE*, and the other of course, *WHO*. Moon just beat the shit out of them for fifteen minutes nonstop.

Peter Townshend ("He's a God in England," Eric Clapton said to me before they went on) leaped in the air, spinning his arms wildly and just being the most generally uninhibited guitar player ever seen in these parts. Roger Daltrey broke a total of eighteen microphones over the full run of the show. And John Entwhistle would just lean up against his amp taking it all in.

They reached the modulation part of the instrumental, and Townshend spun his guitar in the air, caught it, and smashed it

"Waiter, there's a bat in my glass." Greenwich Village, '66: Steve, Danny, Al, Andy, Roy. PHOTO: ALICE OCHS.

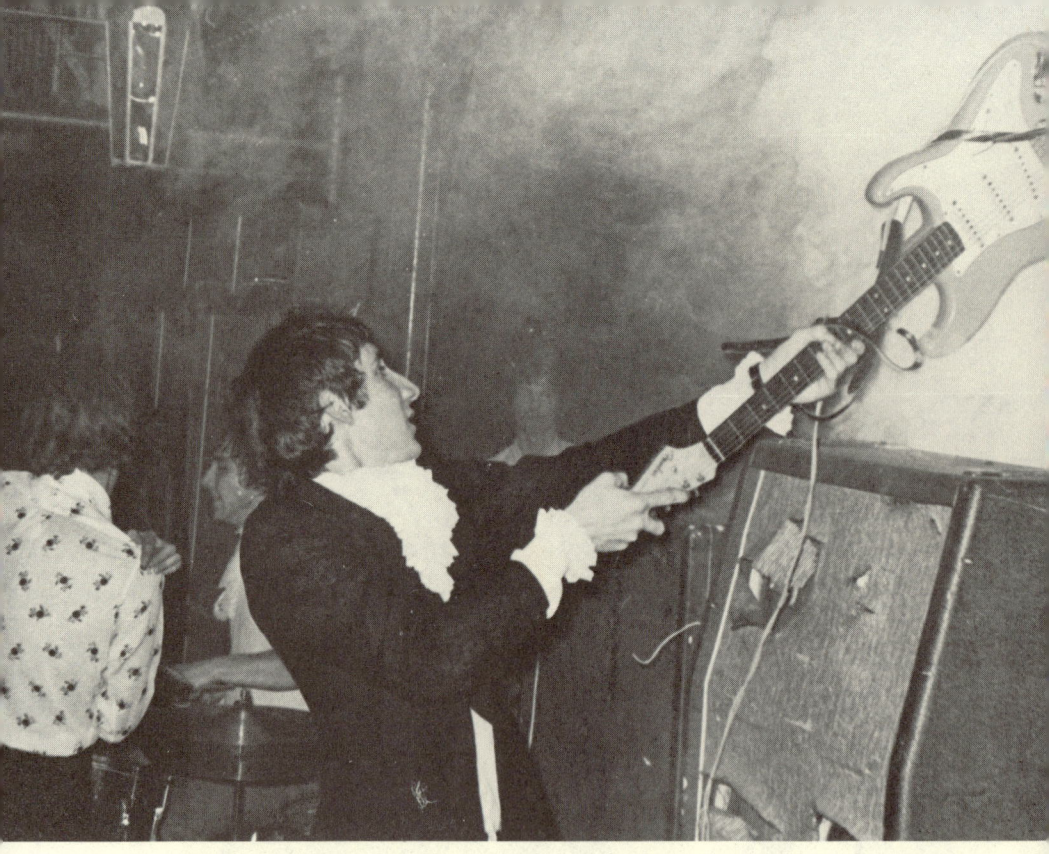

Pete Townshend attempts to rescue children from a neighbor's flaming amp in Surrey. PHOTO: AL KOOPER COLLECTION.

I am awakened by Steve during a Blues Project recording session. Andy attempts to hide his nosepicking behind a microphone, while Danny watches in utter disbelief. PHOTO: AL KOOPER COLLECTION.

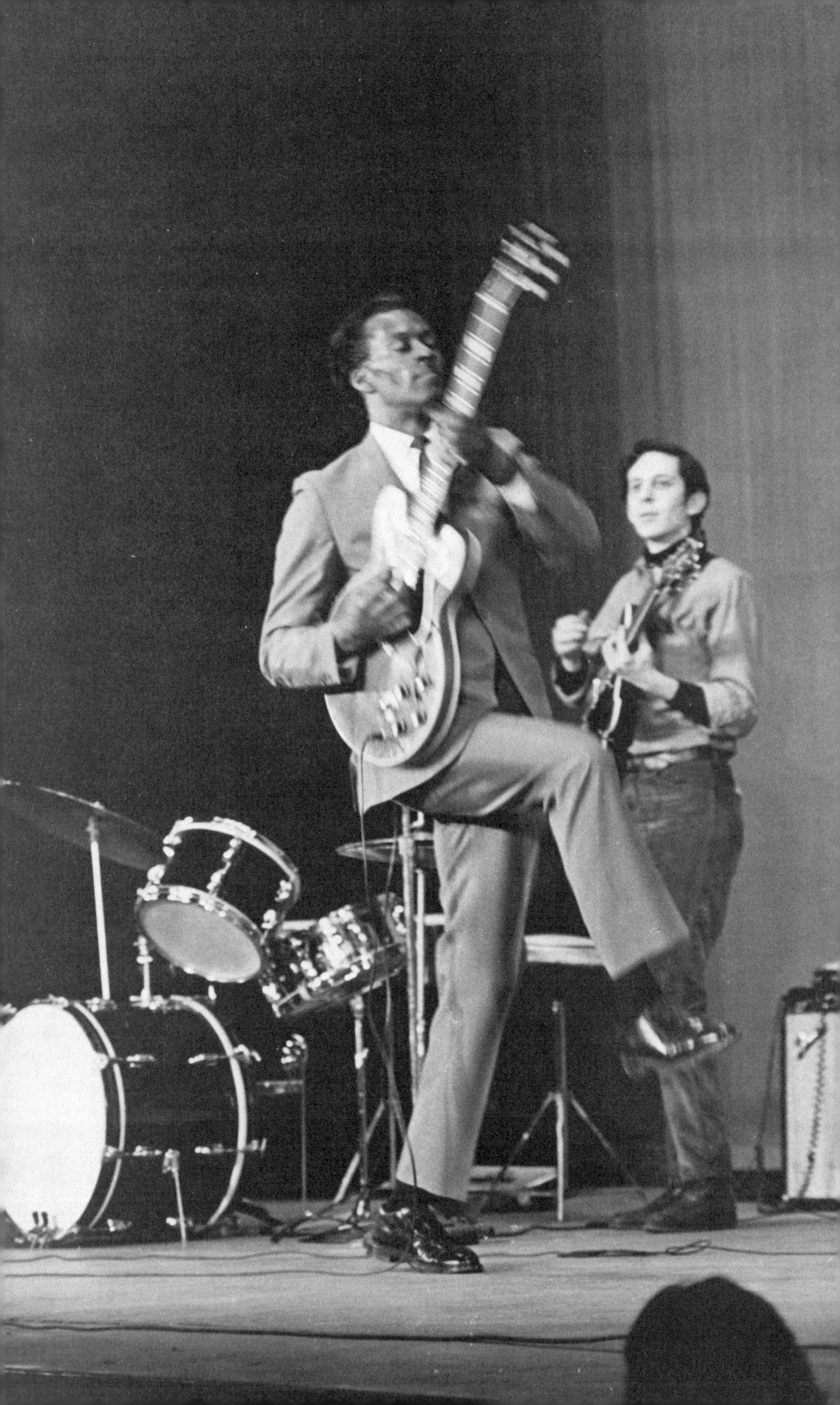

into a placebo amp. No cracks in his Strat, so he aimed for the mikestand. *Whackkkkk!* Crack Number 1. Then the floor. *Whommmpppp!* The guitar is in three or four pieces and he's still got signal coming out of it! All of a sudden Moon kicks his entire drumkit over, and the curtain rings down in a cloud of artificial smoke.

Just then I realized my heart was beating three times its normal speed. I figure as a critic of that show, my elecrocardiogram was the best testimonial I could have offered. Between shows their roadie, Bob Pridden, would glue drums and guitar bits together in the dressing room, all the while constructing smoke bombs and signing microphone repair bills. He had his hands full to say the least. For The Who it was business as usual, even if it was at fifteen minutes a clip.

Wilson Pickett was a strong figure in the R&B world, racking up one number one hit after another and creating many classics ("In the Midnight Hour," "Mustang Sally," "I'm a Midnight Mover," "I Found a Love," and later a great version of Free's "Fire and Water"). He was interested in underground music, and this was the first time he had encountered it firsthand, so he hung out with everyone as much as he could.

Mike Bloomfield and Barry Goldberg came down to catch the show one night. Mike had just quit Butterfield's group and was scouting new musicians for a concept he had for a band. While listening to Pickett's set he became hopelessly infatuated with the playing of Wilson's eighteen-year-old drummer. Bloomers took a shot and stole that drummer right out of Pickett's hand and band. For young Buddy Miles it was a gamble, but a relief from the chitlin circuit that had occupied most of his eighteen years.

So many incestuous things going on. Little did Buddy know that years later when he would front his own band, he would call upon Jim McCarty, the guitar player who was with Mitch Ryder at the show, to join *his* group. Little did Mandala know how they would divide and make a name for themselves individually (Dom Troiano joined the James Gang, Penti Glan and Josef Chiriowski would later provide powerful backup for Lou Reed and Alice Cooper.)

After the last show every night, those who could stand up would make it over to Steve Paul's club and jam all night. Many incredible nights of music went down during that week. It was a memorable show.

•

Finally, we had our big showdown with the Butterfield Gang from Chicago. It was on our home turf. They muscled in on the Cafe Au GoGo, and what could we do? We had to face 'em head on. So for one weekend in 1967, we were on the same bill at the club. It was the first time we had ever squared off against each other on stage. We were primed and they were primed. We alternated headline status each show.

After our first set Bloomfield came into our dressing room; "We heard you guys were shit and played real pussy. Well, it ain't true. You kicked ass out there and we can dig it." We still tried to get up there and kick *their* ass, but it was evenly paced through the whole gig. It was incredible. We would get up and play a hot set and they would play a burner. We would slip and play a fucked-up one, they would go out and die. The weekend culminated in a massive jam during the last set on the last night. The gunfight was over and no one had been injured.

•

I was expanding my horizons and growing in many directions. For one thing, I couldn't understand why we couldn't make records that sounded as good as those other ones on the radio. I knew it was just a matter of concept and time spent in the studio. I'd just written a Top-Forty-type song that I knew the band could do in a way that would endear us to those 45-buying teenies out there and give us the exposure we needed. I convinced Tom Wilson to let us take a *whole day* just to record this one song. To his credit, Danny was docile, and though he hated this kind of musical gesture, he played what was required and even pitched in on the background vocals.

We were in the studio from 11:00 AM to 7:00 PM. We worked

The gunfight in progress: Andy, Elvin, Danny, and Butter. PHOTO: ALICE OCHS.

Al, Bloomers, and Kalb pretending to play together. PHOTO: ALICE OCHS.

out the arrangement beat by beat, bar by bar, until it fit the confining time limit of the 45. Wilson would let us go for awhile, then come in and channel us if we got on the wrong track. It was a key day for me. I was thinking Motown when I put on my organ part, Beatles when I played the Kooperfone solo, and I was trying to imagine myself as a freaked-out Mark Lindsay when I sang the lead vocal. That oughta cover all the bases, I thought. But most of all it was liberation day in the studio and from then on, no one could ever rush me thru three takes again. The song we cut, "No Time like the Right Time," came out and actually made the singles charts (a first for us and, unfortunately, a last) and *soared* to Number 73 on the Top One Hundred. (Well, maybe *it glided.*) But mainly, it was the beginning of the end for the band because Danny hated it as much as I loved it.

Progress, dammit, that's what I was into. I wanted to augment the band with three horns, and got turned down cold by everyone. Danny said we hadn't scratched the surface of what we could do in our current configuration, so why add people and raise our overhead even more? I had no comeback for his financial argument, but the die was cast. I had been writing songs that I knew were best expressed with horn backups. Danny was on my case for trying to sing like a black man. Sort of hypocritical, being that he was as guilty as I was. I mean, he didn't sound like a middle-class kid from Mount Vernon when he sang "Goin' Down Louisiana." For that matter, I don't think he ever *went* down Louisiana. I love you, Danny. We were young and foolish.

Rehearsals were becoming apathetic and nonproductive. The other guys were, in my estimation, getting lazy and fat, as they say in the biz. I realized I couldn't play somebody else's blues anymore. I had my own blues, and it was time to sing *my* song, not Jimmy Reed's or Muddy Waters! All this pressure was building up inside me with no outlet, compounded by my usual high drug intake.

Something had to give.

One night, in the middle of a blistering argument with my wife, Joan, all of a sudden I shut up and became sort of catatonic. Didn't say a word for four days. It was like a dam cracking, except that it was me cracking (up). I actually felt a snap occur inside my head and then relief at not having to speak anymore. It scared Joan. I mean I just sat propped up in bed all day, staring at the wall, real quiet.

I remember they sent Sid Bernstein around to see me. He put his hand on my hand and talked to me, almost oblivious to the fact I wasn't replying.

"Rest up, kiddo," he recited. "There's absolutely nothing you have to do this week, so there's no pressure if you just lay back and take it easy. By next weekend, you'll be fine and we'll play that Chicago gig."

I couldn't believe him. I wanted to jump up and scream, *"It's over, you motherfucker! It's over! Look what's become of me. I can't stand another minute of this shit. Go away!"* Of course, he had no way of knowing this; he just thought I was tired. Sid was so busy keeping us afloat businesswise, he couldn't see the heavy emotional undertow going on in the band.

When I finally started talking, I called up my dad and borrowed $2,000 from him. First time I ever asked him for anything. Blew his mind. He did not fail me, even though he had to borrow it from someone else 'cause he was a little short at the time. Not much, mind you; about 5' 7". Joan and I quickly packed it up and caught the next plane to California to "rest." Whew!

·

PHOTO: LINDA EASTMAN MCCARTNEY.

PHOTO: JIM MARSHALL.

5

If You're Going to California, Wear Some Brains in Your Head

Los Angeles had always seemed to me a kind of mythic place where that magical "it" was always happening first, whether it was sun-baked beaches in the pages of *Look* magazine or bands like the Byrds and Buffalo Springfield that were providing the freshest American alternative to the English stranglehold on rock 'n' roll. The music business had begun its slow migration from Broadway in New York to the Coast, and residence in L.A. was becoming a symbol of affluence. Sort of like, well, you've graduated from New York High School, now four years in the Los Angeles College of "not so" Hard Knocks, and then maybe we'll ship you to London for your post-graduate work.

The paradox was that I found the thought of residing in that California "paradise" depressing and more than a little like giving up. The New York sensibility has always regarded California with suspicion; if your system is geared to New York's nonstop adrenaline rush, the relaxed California life-style can seem as if you're playing a 45 record at 16. It's like if New Yorkers want to follow that slow a pace, they retire to Florida. My impression was that it was almost too easy to get by in L.A. and, although my overloaded mental and emotional circuits definitely needed the rest, I couldn't really feel comfortable about a move that I subconsciously equated with resigning to a condominium in St. Petersburg. Nonetheless, I'd barely gotten it together to roll out of bed before I was winging my way westward.

Joan and I checked into the Hollywood Sunset Hotel (then the most favored L.A. pop hotel and now a retirement apartment complex) and fanned our address books in search for anyone who might put us up. Joan had a friend in Oakland named Anne, who was gracious enough to offer us lodging for as long as we needed it. So off to Oakland we flew, only to be confronted with a scene that we weren't even slightly prepared to cope with.

What Anne had neglected to mention was that her house was the number-one crashpad in the Bay Area. Joining us in our northern California holiday retreat were every speed freak in San Francisco, an eccentric rock band and their various women, and Anne's old man, whose sole claim to fame was that he had once managed a fairly popular rock group. Talk about horror shows! This scene was like a distillation of all the negative stereotypes that the media was then promulgating about the hippie phenomenon. If this was the wave of the future, get me back to the Brill Building!

In order to get to our sleeping quarters, we had to boost ourselves up through the kitchen ceiling and into the attic, which had just enough space to allow you to walk around in a small circle hunched over. Our newlyweird suite came furnished with a single blood-stained mattress that had no sheets, compliments of the management. Well, I admit that it wasn't the Beverly Hills Hotel (no matter *what* hallucinogenic drug you were on) but, I mean, they didn't even ask us to *chip in for food!*

God, it was depressing. I'd use up the days making small talk with the endless procession of wasted faces that passed through the house, just generally taking up my own space without intruding on anyone else's. At night I'd sit up in that attic and crumble into Mr. Hyde. It was *de rigueur* to cry oneself to sleep; it seemed to suit the environment. When they film this part of the movie, it'll be in sepia.

This cockroach sidetrip was getting us nowhere, and was not

exactly the kind of rehabilitation I'd had in mind when we fled to California. I mean, it told me everything I wanted to know about a certain kind of life I *didn't* want to lead, but in that respect was just another addition to an already crowded list. I certainly wasn't doing too much to straighten out my considerably twisted brain. Each day I'd twist it a little more in an attempt to find an escape from my escape. My address book had burns on the pages from all the time I spent staring at the names and numbers in it over and over again.

Finally, we lucked out. I chanced a call to David Anderle, an old acquaintance in L.A., and he consented to have us as his Hollywood houseguests. Relief!

David Anderle was an unemployed record person I'd met while in the Blues Project. He had been a promotion man for MGM in L.A., and during the convention at which we'd played, he was kind enough to take me to his doctor for a much-needed (feel free to use your imagination) penicillin shot. What I needed now was a shot of privacy, and his home was a welcome syringe.

At various times since the MGM days, David had managed a singer named Danny Hutton (who almost made it big with a local hit, "Roses and Rainbows," and later went all the way with "Three Dog Night") babysat for Brian Wilson of The Beach Boys (taking care of *him* as opposed to his kids), encouraged Van Dyke Parks, and painted fabulous portraits of the people that moved him. David's first love was painting, and anyone who's ever seen his work comes away wondering what strange allure the record business could hold for a man so artistically gifted.

He resided in a lovely facade up in the Hollywood Hills, which featured a neat fake waterfall in the backyard. It was a vast improvement on our Oakland accommodations, and we were *almost* happy. But I was still running blind, and David picked up on it right away.

One day, he took me down the hill to an office on Sunset Boulevard where all these people were engaged in the planning of a pop festival to be held in Monterey in four weeks' time. Quite a crew: Lou Adler, Ben Shapiro, Alan Pariser, Guy

Webster, Tom Wilkes, Derek Taylor, and the familiar face of Edward Herbert Beresford (Chip) Monck.

I'd known Chip from the Dylan days in New York. He always did the lights and staging at the Newport Folk and Jazz Festivals. He put in the Tiffany lamps at the Derby Steak House in the Village (his first New York gig) and redesigned the Village Gate jazz club. He was a welcome slice of east coast reality.

I sat down to chat it up with him and he was soon asking my advice on what kind of instruments and amplifiers to rent. In short order he had me on the phone making calls and assisting him. David ducked out the door, and before you could say, "I've never engaged in this kind of thing before," I'd become Assistant Stage Manager of the Monterey Pop Festival.

The job channeled my insanity. I would come there every day, get on the phone, and order and connive equipment. The fever, dedication, and enthusiasm of those present hit you in the face the moment you walked through the door. Derek Taylor, fresh from a P.R. stint with the Beatles, was on hand as a general antidote to any unnecessary uptightness. Lou Adler and Alan Pariser took his shots straightfaced; I guess 'cause they were immune to him, but he could reduce anyone else to instant giggles if they got too far into a jam. He made a living out of that in the sixties and saved a great many people from falling into that dreaded abyss called seriousness. A transplanted fixture on the L.A. scene, it would have been impossible to pull the festival off without him. And for me, his presence was just what the doctor would've ordered if I'd had the sense to see one.

Tom Wilkes and Guy Webster handled the graphics and put together a memorable program book. A classic time capsule of that period, it was unfortunately not made available after the festival. The only surviving copy I know about was on Steve Katz's coffee table, but his house burned down, so maybe that one isn't even around. I wrote a poem that was included in it; they encouraged off-the-wall contributions of that sort. I used to fantasize putting out a book of poetry, so I carried a notebook around on the road and free-associated my way through the

Blues Project in its pages. Only two of the poems were ever published: "Paramount As Abc" (Monterey program book) and "Line Her Nodes" (the notes to my first solo album; more about that later). After my plane crash I'm sure you'll be able to pick up a copy of the rest of them; I've left strict instructions.

Lou Adler was real surprised to see me, as he'd booked the Project for the Festival.

"What are you doing here?"

"I quit the band."

"But I've got them booked."

"They'll be there."

"Are they any good?"

"Of course, I was only one-fifth."

He was easily persuaded to keep them on the show. (I was curious to see what they were gonna do, anyway.) Chip and I were snowing Fender and Hammond in an attempt to convince them to lend us equipment free of charge in return for credit in the program book and on the TV show (ABC owned the rights to the festival). We were in touch with the road managers from every group to make sure that their specifications could be met. In other words, no surprises for anyone except the audience. This was gonna be a smoothie even if the prefestival madness was anything but smooth.

•

Back at the house, meanwhile, it was midway through the six-day Arab-Israeli War, and David was locked into the TV, cheering his race on to victory. Joan, my second wife, was trapped in the house by her inability to face reality and take a driving test. Little mention is made of our relationship in these pages, and with good reason. I think you'd find it boring; it's the kind of inconsequential personal stuff that I'm never interested in when I'm reading someone else's book. Suffice to say that I wasn't treating dear Joan especially well, and she was getting madder each day. I was so caught up in the festival that I was oblivious to everything else, including her anger. But at least by this time my insanity was manifesting itself functionally. When I was working, I was totally coherent. When I wasn't I was simply a lunatic. (People have since told me that they've never been able to tell the difference.)

One day I had lunch with Jac Holzman, the president of Elektra Records and a close friend. Elektra was making a brave plunge into the new music that was hanging in the air, and he asked if I knew anyone suitable to run his West Coast office and studios. I flashed on a great way to pay my rent and immediately suggested Anderle, who I was certain could handle the job admirably. Soon Jac and David were deep into discussions about how Elektra could conquer the world. David put his paints away, and in the course of running the office he wound up producing a few gold albums for Judy Collins. I felt I'd repaid the kindness David had shown me.

BE: Anderle has remained a producer, turning out excellent albums for, among others, Kris Kristofferson, Rita Coolidge, and the Ozark Mountain Daredevils.

The weeks flew by until one morning we woke up and it was the day before the festival. The management had rented a nifty Lear Jet in which to ferry the staff and notables from L.A. to Monterey. Joan and I somehow lost track of the schedule, and late in the day we got a frantic call from the airport.

"Where the hell are you? The plane is waiting, it costs money, bla-bla-bla."

So we raced for the airport in David's car and ended up tearassing onto the charter service runway just like at the end of *Casablanca*, life imitating art.

Ever flown in a Lear Jet? *Real* exciting. It was a five-seater, and its passengers on this shuttle were Alan Pariser, John Phillips, me, Joan, and Brian Jones (late of The Rolling Stones). Brian had just endured a flight from England. Pariser met him at the gate and whisked him through customs and straight to the Lear Jet. He appeared to be convening in the neighborhood of Jupiter.

The earlybird gets the best seat: Al pretending to be Ringo, unidentified flying lady, and Jack Casady, Jefferson Airplane's bassist. PHOTO: JIM MARSHALL.

    We all strapped in and the plane took off immediately. *Almost straight up.* The flight was outrageous. I was at this time already a veteran of the skies, but no kind of commercial flight really prepares you for your first Lear Jet ride. The thing goes so fast that you don't believe it even as it's happening.
    When we landed in Monterey, Brian spoke to me for the first time that evening. "Hi, Al." I don't think he was aware that our introduction had taken place some forty-five minutes before.

And High Al I was. The flight velocity, altitude, or *something* had stoned me good, and I tripped along quietly as we drove into the fair city of Monterey. We ran into some friends we hadn't seen in awhile at the motel, and stayed up all night partying. It was a fitting beginning to the festival weekend.

I made it over to the fairgrounds early the next AM. Chip, who'd been there for five days doing advance work, had it together as usual. I just got on the phone and confirmed everyone for the soundchecks and so forth, filling in the small details. The show began with a set by Canned Heat, and from there it was three days of paradise. And, from an Assistant Stage Manager's perspective, it worked like a bitch. By now reams have been written about Monterey Pop, so you'll excuse me if I don't detail it act by act at this late date.

There were several artists and friends that I was especially looking forward to seeing. While sitting around David Anderle's house that summer, we spent a great deal of time listening to this English album I'd borrowed from Aaron Schroeder; he had recently signed the act for stateside publishing. The trio was fronted by a guitar-playing American expatriate that I'd often marvelled at when he was a part of John Hammond Jr.'s backing group at the Gaslite in New York, and I was anxious to see how he would do in his debut American performance since becoming a European sensation. His name was Jimi Hendrix.

Also on the bill were my old friends from the Murray the K disaster, The Who, and even older friends, Paul Simon and Artie Garfunkel. It was also an opportunity to take in the whole spectrum of West Coast music, from the Los Angeles bands that I already knew and loved (The Byrds, The Buffalo Springfield, and The Mamas and the Papas) to the surging San Francisco wave that, for the most part, I'd only heard *about* (Jefferson Airplane, The Grateful Dead, and Big Brother and the Holding Company, who had a singer named Janis Joplin that *everybody* was raving about. I soon found out why.)

•

To digress a bit now that we've mentioned West Coast music, David Anderle had also been responsible for engineering a

Checking out Hendrix at the Monterey soundcheck. PHOTO: JIM MARSHALL.

"Jeez, you don't *look* English!" PHOTO: JIM MARSHALL.

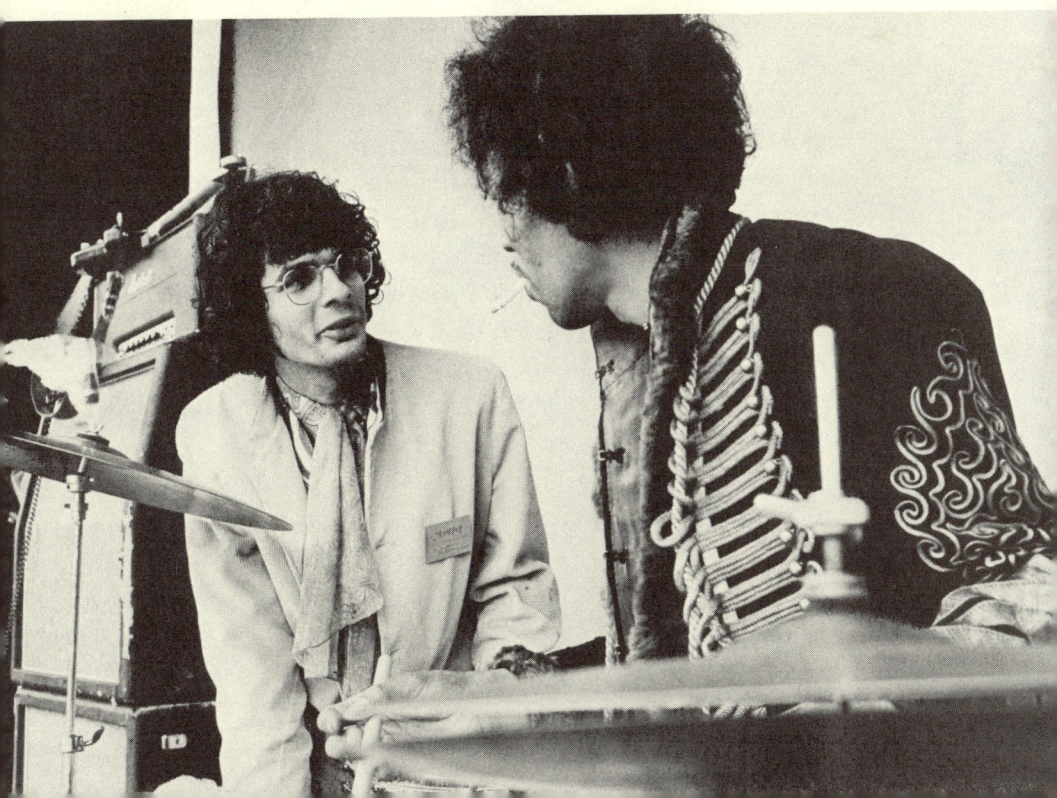

meeting between me and one of my idols, Brian Wilson of The Beach Boys.

BE: When the underground emerged, the popularity of The Beach Boys, who'd been America's favorite sons since the early sixties, faded away. In the new audience's search for cultural validity, they were discarded with the rest of yesterday's values. Feeling the awkwardness of the situation, they backed out of Monterey Pop, even though group leader Brian Wilson was on its board of directors. But musicians and anybody else with honest ears readily acknowledge the group's vanguard status in terms of harmonic creativity and pop sophistication. When he conceived an album called *Pet Sounds* and a single "Good Vibrations," Brian Wilson was hailed by the elite as one of the true masters. It wasn't until the early seventies, when The Beach Boys' popularity resurged, that the general public finally caught up.

So we went up to Brian's house, a sprawling Spanish place in ultra-posh Bel Aire, one evening about a week before he unleashed *Pet Sounds* on the world. He played a test pressing of the record, jumping up and stopping cuts in the middle and starting them over to emphasize his points. He was proud of his accomplishment, maybe even a little show-offish, but I wasn't about to argue. Do you remember the first time *you* heard "God Only Knows?"

Then he sat down at the piano in his living room (which featured a full-on soda fountain where the bar should've been) and gave us two uninterrupted hours of possible variations on "Trees"—you know, the "I think that I shall never see a poem as lovely" thing—which he hoped to have The Beach Boys record. I'd brought along a copy of *Music of Bulgaria,* my fave rave album at the time, and he got blown out by that. Then he blew me out completely by playing a track he was working on and singing along to it live. The song was "Good Vibrations;" 'nuff said. He also played me a rough tape of "Heroes and Villains," which had evolved, I believe, from a Wilson revamping of "You Are My Sunshine." In all it was a great evening; one of the few that really captured all the California magic that the rest of the country imagines from a distance. Thanks for the memories, Brian.

Through all of this, I had been sort of planning my next move; deep in the back of my mind was a band that could put dents in your shirt if you got within fifteen rows of the stage. Like Maynard Ferguson's band from the years 1960–1964, I wanted a horn section that would play *more* than the short adjectives they were delegated in R&B bands. But, on the other hand, a horn section that would play *less* than Count Basie's or Buddy

Vanilla and Chocolate: Harvey Brooks and Buddy Miles, Electric Flagwavers. PHOTO: ALICE OCHS.

Rich's. Somewhere in the middle was a mixture of soul, jazz, and rock that was my little fantasy.

I confided this concept to David Crosby one day, and he sent me to a local club to check out a guitar player he thought would be great for it. I fell out over the guitarist, introduced myself, and explained this concept to him. He thought it was a good idea, but insisted that he was committed to the band he was in. His name was Danny Weiss, and his band was Iron Butterfly. He left soon after that and joined the great but doomed Rhinoceros.

I was turned on to Jim Fielder, who had just been booted out of The Buffalo Springfield, and had played with Frank Zappa's Mothers before that. He was a Texas-born mother of a bass player, and we jammed a lot over at his house in Laurel Canyon. With a drummer friend of his named Sandy Konikoff, we made pretty agreeable music.

Mike Bloomfield was concurrently putting together a horn-type group up north that sounded in rumour exactly like my fantasy. This group was closing the big afternoon show at the festival, so you *know* that that's what I was most interested in. Bloomfield had kidnapped Buddy Miles (from Wilson Pickett's band at that Murray the K show in the last chapter), and together with Harvey Brooks (my boyhood chum) on bass, Barry Goldberg on keyboards, Marcus Doubleday (a descendent of the inventor of baseball, Abner Doubleday) on trumpet, Peter Strazza on tenor sax, and Nick Gravenites on vocals and percussion, they had rehearsed for two or three months up in Marin county, just outside San Fran.

This was their first gig, and they were terrified. Buddy Miles had a suit on fer chrissakes; one of those jobbies like James Brown wore, with no lapels and a shirt and tie! Bloomfield came out and gave one of his great speeches about how we (the audience) were all one and it was all peace, love, and incense, and here's some music by the way.

Heavy drama. But they played great. The crowd went nuts. I was standing backstage with Susie Bloomfield (Michael's wife), and she was crying tears of joy and relief. Buddy Miles came off after playing to his first large, predominantly white audience and he was sweating and crying. And, caught up in the thrill of it all, I was crying. But I was smiling at the same time, because my idea was still intact. Bloomfield's band, soon to be called Electric Flag, was sticking to tradition. They played their tunes in a faithful Stax-Volt tribute to the Memphis sound, and while it was overpowering and gorgeous to see and hear, it was flagrantly derivative. My band would *not* sound like any band that had ever been.

After Monterey folded up its petals, I bummed a ride to San Francisco to waste a few days. Joan had fled back to the Big Apple, in a rage, on the last day of the festival, giving my self-absorbed ass a mucho-deserved stiff boot. Joan Baez was throwing an annual party known as the Big Sur Folk Festival, and I drifted in that direction. I'd played at the previous year's fest as a solo act, and had been invited to perform once again.

The get-together was held on the grounds of the tranquil Esalen Institute, and had maintained a low enough profile to insure that it would be full but not overcrowded. It was as if they'd simply shifted the party from Monterey to Big Sur. Simon and Garfunkel donated their much-in-demand services for free in order to partake in the surroundings and get their hip cards punched one notch further. It was especially nice for me, 'cause I schlepped Jim Fielder and Sandy Konikoff along and took the opportunity to debut some of my new songs. "I Can't Quit Her" and "My Days Are Numbered" went down well with the crowd, adding fuel to my fantasy of a new band.

Since this is the last we see of Sandy Konikoff, I should thank him profusely for working for insulting wages, loving the music, and inventing the sphincterphone. The *what*? Ah, a good story.

Elektra Records West, under the direction of one David Anderle, had opened a secluded recording ranch on the Feather River in northern California so that embryonic talent could have a relaxed environment in which to record and then, the script goes, think kindly enough of Elektra to sign with them if the corporate mouths smiled on their tapes.

BE: One such project, which never quite panned out, was a loose collection of performing songwriters called the Los Angeles Fantasy Orchestra, which numbered among its ranks Jackson Browne and Ned Doheny.

Sandy was the drummer in the ranchband. One night, bongos or congas were desperately desired for a particular song they were recording, but none were to be had, and it would've taken days to have anything shipped to their far-flung location. In a spectacular effort to please, Sandy took a pencil-thin snare drum microphone and inserted it anally, beating out the required rhythm on his belly after the engineer had jacked up the level and added appropriate echo. Not having been present on this historic occasion, I can offer only second-hand information, but I'm told he didn't miss a beat. That was the birth of the sphincterphone. I've heard of putting your ass on the line for a gig, but Sandy, you're ridiculous!

Back at Big Sur, they were offering Simon and Garfunkel, the Chambers Brothers, Judy Collins, and Joan Baez and her sisters Mimi Farina and Pauline Marden (the Baez Brothers, as I was fond of calling them). The three-day hang-out climaxed with the afternoon of the actual performances, which attracted scene fixtures as diverse as Ralph J. Gleason and Bobby Neuwirth and tied it all together with a peace and love ambience that was much easier to believe in in those days.

The only loose end was Al "Not Quite the Life of the Party" Kooper, who insisted on getting depressed in the midst of all these good vibes and wandered off into the woods to have a catatonic flashback. I must've been giving off rank vibes, because Judy Collins came over and asked what was wrong. When I proved incapable of a reply, she took me by the hand and steered me back to my hotel room, where she then endured an all-night crying jag on the part of yours truly. To her credit (and, I've no doubt, extreme discomfort), she was able to talk me down to a somewhat functional frame of mind; just another of the many Big

This photo reminds me of Tina Turner in *Gimme Shelter:* Actually Mimi, one of the famous Baez Brothers singing group. PHOTO: ALICE OCHS.

Al with the leader of the Baez Brothers. PHOTO: JIM MARSHALL.

Ones I owe Judy Collins. (I've glossed over my emotional traumas because, as I said before, that stuff is best left to soap operas. And besides, how can you take *anything* seriously in the paragraph following the sphincterphone?)

The next day I caught a ride to San Francisco and proceeded on to Berkeley. Sally Henderson (the sister of Jill, in whose Cambridge apartment I'd written "Flute Thing") was running the Jabberwock, the club where I'd first met Joan, and she booked me in and gave me room and board. I played solo for the first time since I'd joined the Blues Project; I almost felt like calling myself Al Casey.

Opening the show was another man in limbo at the time, Taj Mahal. I was familiar with Taj from an L.A. band he'd been in called the Rising Sons.

BE: The vaguely legendary Rising Sons included, in addition to Taj, drummer Ed Cassidy, who later went on to form Spirit, and two exceptional guitar players in Ry Cooder and Jessie Ed Davis.

He had a steel National guitar and he had the blues. He dispensed them in such a forthright manner that the stage would be smoking each night after he'd come off, and it took some severe rising to the occasion for me to hold my own on the bill with him. I played my Blues Project favorites and the new songs I was developing and, in retrospect, it was probably one hell of a show, historically speaking, for $3.50.

A nice gesture for history, perhaps, but monetary rewards from this venture weren't enough to sustain me for more than a few days. It was clearly time to face the music, both personally and professionally, back in New York. I caught the first available plane East. I had been gone ten weeks, and had pissed away in excess of two thousand dollars. I had barely enough money in my pockets to get myself home when the plane touched down in New York. *And I didn't even have a tan.*

PHOTO: FRED LOMBARDI, CBS.

6

Bloodstains on the Keyboard or What to Call Your New Band

I arrived in New York, as best as I can recall, during the first week in July of 1967. On the plane ride home, I had constructed a scheme of complex proportions for a) changing my environment, b) getting some cash together, and c) most important of all, putting my dreamband together. I got home and took inventory: no money, no Joanie, no gigs. My fucking rat-infested apartment (I walked in the door from California, to be greeted by the scurry of little feet) on Waverly Place was a depressing base of operations. The one thing I had going for me was friends (not the furry, rodent kind).

I got on someone's phone and called all my friends who were musicians. I got Howard Solomon to give me the Cafe Au GoGo for two nights so I could throw a benefit for *myself*. Then I called Judy Collins, Paul Simon, and Eric Andersen, among others, to ask them if they'd play for nothing as a favor so I could raise enough money to at least *peek* over the top. Well, everybody's real nice and we soon got us a show, folks. We advertised, peddled tickets at reasonable prices, and sold it out in advance!

I decided to get a pickup group together 'cause now I'd gotten the fever and wanted to play at my own show. I got an advance from Howard Solomon and flew Jim Fielder in to play bass (he was all I had to show for that hunk of time spent in

L.A.). Steve Katz knew of a good drummer, and he turned me on to his close friend, Bobby Colomby, who had been playing backup for Eric Andersen and Odetta. Steve came to the first rehearsal to watch and ended up joining on guitar. We rehearsed about five days and worked up most of the new material I had written plus my "hits" from the Project.

The plan was to take the proceeds from the gig, buy a one-way plane ticket to London, and put my band together there. I thought the change of scene would do me good, England being musically charismatic at that time, and I found it romantic to consider myself an "expatriate." Not a bad scheme; it looked great on paper.

The shows go on, and it's incredible seeing Judy Collins, sweat pouring off her (as Howie's air-conditioning rudely bites the bag the night she plays), appearing in a small club again, showering her rekindled intimacy and perspiration on a loving audience. Everybody in the Village came down to play; there were jams and too many acts to even fit in at each show. It made me very proud and thankful that people can be so thoughtful and generous. We stretched it out through a third night and then it was over.

Six sold-out shows. July 27, 28 and 29. That's 1,800 people at four dollars a head. You figure it out. So the next day, I'm sitting in Howie Solomon's office and he hands me a check for five hundred dollars. He says the rest went to expenses—paying the help, advertising, free admission to many "friends," and a thousand miscellaneous etceteras. My shot was blown. I didn't even have enough for the *plane ticket*. I was stuck in New York, my lady had runned off with another musician, and after what everyone did for me at the benefit, there was no way I could dial a number in New York and say "please" or "could you" or even "what's happening?"

•

I was sitting in my apartment, well into a state of shock, when the doorbell rang and in marched Katz, Fielder, and Colomby. "Al, we heard what happened. But why don't you add hornplayers to our existing rhythm section? We already know how good it can sound, and Jim's offered to move permanently to New York."

Hmmmmmmmm.

"Well," I said, mulling this over. I couldn't realistically imagine rising to any great heights with Steve, who had tagged along and was, at best, an adequate guitarist. But there was virtually no choice. Right now, it was them or starve-o. "There is only one condition," I said. "I know exactly what I want to do, and in the Blues Project I was prevented from doing it because of majority rule. It's got to be set up in front that I'm the leader and will define the band's repertoire and arrangements and anything else to do with musical policies."

No hesitation. "Oh yeah! Right on, Al baby."

I should have known better.

Bobby was the only one who had any links to horn players, because they hadn't played a role in the rest of our musical lives up to that point. Bobby said there was one guy from his neighborhood who was a local legend and had been Bobby's boyhood idol. His name was Fred Lipsius, and Bobby set about attempting to contact him.

Fred showed up at rehearsal a few days later, and I couldn't believe it. Sam straight. Short hair, square clothes, the whole bit. Then he unpacks his alto and starts playing and that's *it* for me. I don't give a fuck what this guy looks like, he can play that motherfuckin saxophone and make it *cry* f'chrissakes!! We played him all my tunes, and he said he was in.

Freddie was as sweet and innocent as anyone could possibly be, and a corruption process was essential. He'd *never* listened to rock 'n' roll; he was a hard-core jazz cat but had soul in huge doses. We used to force-feed him marijuana and make him listen to *Sgt. Pepper* with headphones on. He got the picture, and pretty soon we had us a rockin' alto player.

Freddie was put in charge of recruiting the horn section and we devised a strategy for choosing the right members. Freddie and I wrote the initial arrangements together and purposely overwrote them. That is, we had the horns playing practically all the way through each song, and in *every* chart executing difficult passages a player might normally confront once in ten charts. We decided that anyone who could play these charts and still have any desire to be in the band (thinking he would have to do this every night) was OK in our book.

We held open auditions and went through quite a collection of characters. Schoolteachers, junkies, real old dudes, pimps, winos; it was an assortment of people we didn't normally spend a whole lot of time around. Hornplayers had been sadly neglected in the white rock 'n' roll business. Little did I know that this band was gonna change that.

While we were trying to find the right guys, I took the rhythm section into the studio and cut three demos to play for record companies in order to sell the band. I hired two trumpet players (studio cats) and overdubbed them so that the final sound was us and four trumpets. We recorded "I Can't Quit Her," "My Days Are Numbered" (which are both featured on our first album), and a song I co-wrote with a friend named Tony Powers, "I Need to Fly." The overall effect was surprisingly close to our goal, and certainly indicative of what someone could expect to get if they purchased us. We needed $40,000 to keep the band alive while an album was in progress and, unlike our lack of affinity with the record company in the Blues Project, a humanistic relationship with the corporate fathers. The forty Gs turned off Jerry Wexler at Atlantic (they are not known for gambling large sums of monies on embryonic talent), although I must say he was into the music. Mo Ostin of Warner Brothers came over to (or should I say braved) my ratpad to listen to the demos, but his follow-up from California seemed apathetic.

Bill Gallagher at Columbia and his soon-to-be successor, Clive Davis, were real interested. They had attended the Monterey Pop Festival and were now turned on to the dollar potential of the underground market. Clive set up a luncheon date for the two of us. I met him in his office at CBS. I was real scruffy, unshaven, and a true test of any executive's desire to sign the band was if they would dare to appear in public with me. Clive seemed unfazed by the prospect, and we adjourned down the block to the Hickory House, a pencil-pushers' haven on West Fifty-second Street. I had asked that we go somewhere where I could order eggs, because, although it was *his* lunchtime, it was *my* breakfast.

We were ushered in and seated immediately. Along comes one of those inevitable waiters-with-an-accent cartoons who hands us menus and waits for our order. I didn't see any kind of eggs on the menu, and I could immediately see that this was gonna be trouble. I mentioned as much to Clive and suggested going somehwere else, but he must have had a piece of the place or something 'cause he wouldn't budge.

"Just tell the waiter what you'd like," he said.

Here goes nothin', I thought to myself. "Three eggs over easy, buttered whole-wheat toast, and a large milk," I said to the waiter.

"*Escargot?*" he says, trying to figure what this long-haired asshole is talking about. I recited the order slowly once again, and he was even more confused. I flashed an "I told you so" look Clive's way. Clive, ever eager to sign a new band, leaps from his seat and, while I'm wondering if I can quietly slip under the table, grabs the waiter's jacket collar with both hands· and screams, "He wants three eggs over easy with buttered toast and a glass of milk!"

I didn't get whole-wheat toast, but we signed with Columbia anyway.

•

After exhausting auditions, the lineup of the band was firm: Steve, Bobby, Jimmy, Freddie, and me, plus Randy Brecker and Jerry Weiss (trumpets and flugelhorns), and Dick Halligan (trombone). The experiment even had a name. Barry Imhoff, who used to work under Howie Solomon at the Au GoGo, opened up an ambitious club of his own called Generation. It was the Cafe Au GoGo minus the sleaze, although it was eventually ambushed by its less-than-fashionable Eighth Street downtown address.

Every night after the other clubs closed, jam sessions with personnel that would make your stare hand on end took place until de sun came up.

One particular night, Jimi Hendrix, BB King, myself, and an unidentified drummer were going at it all night at the GoGo. (Generation and Solomon were in competition over who would have the *best jams*, even.) When we finished playing, they put the house lights up and somebody says: "Christ! Look at the organ! There's blood all over the keyboard!" Sure enough, I had cut my hand playing, and in the state of bliss induced by my compatriots' sound had not felt a thing. What a great album cover, I thought. No. What a great name for the band. *Blood Sweat & Tears!* And that was it.

We then began serious rehearsals in a two-platoon system: I would rehearse the rhythm section, and Freddie would put the hornplayers through their paces at separate workouts. Every three days we would rehearse the whole band together, see how the pieces fit, and polish it until it shone. After six weeks of intense preparation, we were ready to whip it on y'all.

Somewhere around the last week in November 1967, as far as I can recall, we debuted at the Au GoGo, opening the show for Moby Grape. It was the scariest night of my life. The horns had not yet fully memorized their parts, so our roadies built a giant music stand to set out in front of them. A first for rock, no doubt.

BE: Guys reading music onstage. Jeez, I didn't think guys that played rock 'n' roll *could* read music.

The place was packed with press and Moby Grape fans. I've always felt that those people are sitting there just itching for you to fall on your ass, and that that's where the only real drama comes from. Not whether you were good, but whether you stepped on your dick or not. Whatever they expected, we played a burning set right down their throats. No mistakes. And all new material that no one had heard before. That's hard for an audience to digest, but we pulled it off. After it was over, I was

Steve Katz, Jim Feilder, Jerry Weiss, Fred Lipsius, Bobby Colomby, Dick Halligan, Randy Brecker, and Flowerman; also known as BS&T Volume I. PHOTO: DON HUNSTEIN, CBS.

not the only one with tears in his eyes backstage. The band was off the ground, and it looked like it was gonna fly.

I decided to get John Simon, the guy who produced "Fakin' It" for Simon and Garfunkel (their most avant garde single, doncha think?), to produce our album. I had played "I Can't Quit Her" for John when I first wrote it, and he said if I ever recorded the song, he'd like to produce it. Well, I was ready. We needed a producer who *knew* his music, and unfortunately there weren't too many around that fit that description.

John came to hear us live and loved it. We had a producer, and we were almost ready for the studio. John took us in one day and had us cut our whole repertoire live in one take, just to use as reference. He and I then spent the next two weeks at his house, playing the tape and editing the material in such a way that it would make some kind of sense on a phonograph record. He would say, "That trumpet part there is shit. It's gonna have to go." I'd say, "Well, what have you got that's better?" and we'd kick it around until the right part developed. When it did, we both knew it.

John picked what songs went on the album. They weren't necessarily the ones I would've picked, but I needed to step outside of the situation somehow. I was not keen on "I Can't Quit Her" (which turned out to be one of the most popular) or "My Days Are Numbered" because they were both taxing to my limited vocal capabilities, but John got them on the record and coaxed the best vocals that were possible out of me.

BE: If we were writing a textbook history of rock 'n' roll, John Simon would have to receive special notice not only for producing this BS&T album, but for immediately following it with the brilliant debut album of The Band, *Music From Big Pink*.

AK: Don't forget *Cheap Thrills* by Big Brother.

Meanwhile, I was churning out newer material. One night I finished a song that knocked me on my ass. Where most of my

The brass monster limbers up: Freddy, Dick, Jerry, and Randy, Columbia Studios, 1967. PHOTO: SANDY SPEISER, CBS.

songs are blues influenced and draw on fairly obvious roots from my background, this new one was strangely original. It had its own feeling and owed nothing to anything in my record collection. I called everyone in the band up and urged them over to my house to hear the new composition. When my audience was assembled, I played it to them and they loved it.

"What are you gonna do with it though, Al?" said Bobby Colomby.

"I wanna put it on the album. It says a lot about my growth as a writer, and I'd like people to pick up on that," I responded with a typical naiveté.

"But the band can't—I mean horns, and drums, and shit would fuck that song up. We can't do it on the album," countered Colomby.

I got trouble here, I'm thinkin' to myself. "I want to do it by myself. Maybe with ten or twelve strings or something. It'll give the record some variety and a change of pace."

Pause. Then Bobby again. "But that wouldn't be *the band*, Al. It's not what *the band* is."

That was it. I lost my temper and my cool. "Look. We made a deal, or did you forget? It's my band. But that's not what I'm talking about. I'm a member of the band. So if I step out on one track out of eleven, it's still the band 'cause I'm *in* the fucking band. The only difference is that we can't perform *one* song from the album when we play live. Big fucking deal."

Now Bobby's mad. "There's no way that tune is going on the album and that's it!" He exits with the band members at his heels. The next day it was dumped into John Simon's lap for meditation. He slept on it and two days later called me to tell me it was thumbs up in my direction. We would use twelve strings, and he and I would write the arrangement. The song was called "The Modern Adventures of Plato, Diogenes, and Freud." It was a stream of consciousness lyric about this psychatrist I knew of, an admirer of Timothy Leary, who used drugs in his sessions and had sexual relations with all his women patients. (Made me wanna change my line of work.) Anyway, the decision to include the song on the album was the first step in my departure from the band, only I wasn't aware of it at the time.

Another song which I had just finished, "I Love You More Than You'll Ever Know," was a split tribute to Otis Redding and James Brown. (The lyrics are a nod to Otis's song "I Love You More Than Words Can Say," and the melody is "reminiscent" of James Brown's "It's a Man's World.") On December 6 ('67), Otis died in a plane crash and it really fucked me up. The next night we began recording the album. I insisted we record "I Love You" first. Nobody objected. We put down a blistering track, and it looked like this was gonna be an easy album to make. We overdubbed Freddie's solo and Steve's fills, and then it was time to put a vocal on it. Everyone was real jumpy about it 'cause on the reference tape, where I sang while the whole band played, my vocal performance had been a little shaky (to put it mildly). Now, everyone (including me) was concerned that the addition of my nickel throat would fuck up this hundred-dollar track. I was prepared for this tension, however; my wife had taught me the first few lines of the song in French. So they lower the lights, and everyone is hanging out in the control room. I'm out in the studio with headphones on. They start recording, and the room is all tensed up. It comes time for my first line and I sing it in French, "*Si je te quitterais.*"

Everyone's hysterical and they stop the tape. That loosened everybody up and we start again. Now my eyes are screwed shut, and I'm thinkin' about Otis and this sounds clichéd as hell, but it's true—I'm saying to myself, "This is for you." And I'm singing. One take. They call me into the booth for a playback and everyone's smiling. I listen to it. It's not great and it's not awful, but no one could say it wasn't *real*. The one thing I had going for me was that I *believed* the words of every song I had to sing on the album. If I picked somebody else's song, it was because I was moved emotionally by it.

I sang Randy Newman's "Just One Smile." I got that from *Gene Pitney* of all people; it was on one of his early albums. (He did a great job on it.) I picked "Without Her" by Harry Nilsson, my favorite "outside" song at the time. I had a 45 of it that was just about worn out. I had no idea who the guy was, but the baroque arrangement and superb voice did me in. The words were entirely relatable. We turned it into a bossa nova. Later, the song would become a standard, and such hippies as Jack Jones and Herb Alpert would record their own renditions of it. "So Much Love" was a Carole King–Gerry Goffin tune that I'd heard by Percy Sledge and Ben E. King. I did a lot of rewriting on it (changed the words in the second verse, left out half the bridge, and changed the melody to the second half of the bridge) and my arrangement was considerably different from the original.

Steve needed another song to sing, so I turned him on to Tim Buckley's "Morning Glory." Freddie and I wrote a Bob Dylan–

Curtis Mayfield (not so strange bedfellows) arrangement, and Steve loved it. He wrote a little ditty called "Meagan's Gypsy Eyes," which was about his *brief* relationship with Mimi Farina, though he named it after Alice Ochs's daughter. Freddie, Steve, and Bobby wrote the arrangement of that one. John secured this weird organ (an Allen Explorer) from Carroll Music for me to play on, and it gave the song quite an individual sound.

When Steve was putting the vocal on, we convinced him to hold his Adam's apple between his thumb and forefinger and shake it up and down to simulate fast tremolo on a guitar amp. In truth, it was mostly just to see him standing in the studio all by himself shaking his Adam's apple. We were all in tears in the control room. So much laughing, in fact, that I had a lunatic flash and quickly slipped out of my clothes, snuck into the studio on all fours and tackled him from behind in the middle of one of his vocals. He didn't think that was too funny. (I guess it's not always easy being in a band with somebody like me!)

I wrote another song which was sort of a tongue-in-cheek paean to life in the woods called "House in the Country." Its horn entrance is extremely high-pitched and was difficult to record, as the boys had to contort their faces to hit some of the higher notes, but they got it inside of an hour. A few days after that we were putting percussion on the track, and working with an engineer who was filling in for our regular guy, Lou Waxman. Lou's job was to run the tape machines, making sure the right tracks were in record and playback. So Bobby's in the studio with headphones and a tambourine, and John says "OK, roll it." The tape starts rolling, but we didn't hear anything. All of a sudden this middle-aged engineer jumped up and slammed the machine off. Like a deranged player out of *Othello*, he paced up and down screaming, "Oh my God! Oh my God!"

John and I are looking at each other trying to figure out if he has erased the whole song or what. John played it back to check, with this guy having a nervous breakdown all the while, but it turned out that he'd only erased *the horns* from that really hard beginning part. It was a drag, but it wasn't a disaster. It just meant an hour's work some other day. Once we established this fact, you'd think the guy would cool out or somethin'. Nope. He was going nuts. By then, all Simon and I could do was laugh at this guy. He phoned for a replacement and went home in a state of shock. (I guess it wasn't easy working with *us*?)

As the album neared completion, we brought in a string section to spice up some of the songs and put the backup on my solo song. I came up with the idea of having an overture on the record, and John and I wrote a satiric medley based on the themes from all of the songs. I'm not sure, but I think we had the first rock record with an overture. It was certainly the first with an underture.

We recorded the overture and it sounded legit, which was far from our intentions. John asked Bobby, who had this ridiculous laugh, to laugh all the way through the tune (one minute and thirty-two seconds), so people would know for sure that we weren't serious. Bobby went in, started laughing and discovered that it's not as easy as it might sound. His peculiar laugh is very high-intensity, and he could only get about fifteen seconds on tape at a time. So we kept backtracking until about an hour later, we had a complete track of Bobby's insane laughter.

After laughing hysterically for over an hour, he walked into the control room out of breath. His face was sort of an iridescent green as he sat down on the couch. We listened to the playback and everyone was howling along with his laugh track. As the playback ended, Bobby leaned over and threw up, then fell asleep on the couch for the rest of the night. He had OD'd on laughter. Probably the first such casualty in recording history.

To get atmosphere for the opening and closing of "House in the Country" we needed some down-home ambience; a pastoral sound setting to complement the song's theme. We took a poll and found we could imitate a number of woodsy animals amongst ourselves, so we filled up eight tracks with Bobby the frog, Freddie the bird, Al the goat 'n' goose, and Steve the horse. It actually achieves that country feeling, but it was hard to keep from breaking up while we were doing it. I kept thinking to myself, "Grown men did this!" Then we got a bunch of our friends' kids to sing on the end, highlighted by Bobby Colomby's nephew, who looked at everyone coaxing him to sing, and blurted out "I don't wanna!" We kept *that* on the record. From the first note of "I Love You More Than You'll Ever Know" to the last mix on "So Much Love" took a grand total of two weeks. On December 22, 1967, we finished our first album.

Still we had no title and no cover idea. Initially, we wanted to call it *How I Spent My Summer Vacation*, and even went as far as to shoot a cover in various summer-fun regalia. It proved too silly for the album's contents, however. I racked my brain for weeks until I came up with an interesting idea. There's a semifamous poster of a Telly Savalas-looking fellow with a freshly lit cigarette sitting with a young boy in short pants on his lap. The lad has his exact face; a minor trick photography effect, but extremely effective in this situation. The photo was shot by one of my idols, Alfred Gescheidt, one of the deans of darkroom technique in trick photography.

At my insistence, Bob Cato, Columbia's art director, put in a call to Gescheidt, but he was unavailable. What we did then was to duplicate the poster idea of the man and boy using the members of the band. The album was called *Child Is Father to the Man*. Bob Cato shot the cover himself, but the credit on the album reads: "Cover Photo by Bob Cato après Al Gescheidt." Credit where credit is due.

•

The album came out to fairly good reviews, and Columbia sent us on a ten-city promotion tour. This was where we played to the press of each city and talked on countless radio stations about ourselves and our new album. We played in Boston, opening to Janis Joplin and Big Brother. In Cleveland, we opened the show for Canned Heat. In Detroit, we were opposite Iggy & The Stooges, and in Chicago, The Byrds. In L.A., we headlined over a then-fledgling Blues Image. In San Francisco, Bill Graham put us in Winterland trapped in a staggering show: Jeremy & The Satyrs, James Cotton, and Cream. We held our own and got good reviews. The Family Dogg headlined us the

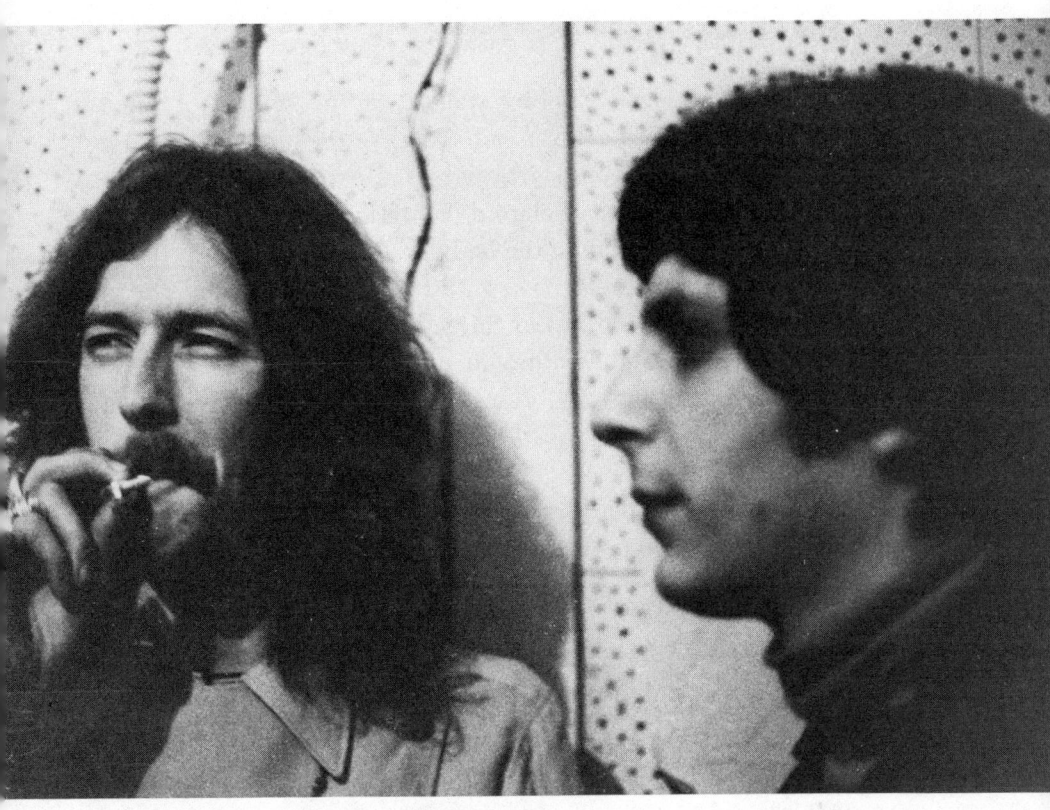

Two guitarists of varying degrees share secrets backstage: Eric Clapton and Steve Katz, Winterland, '68. PHOTO: ALICE OCHS.

next week at the Avalon, with John Handy as support, and we did good business. *Rolling Stone* covered the gig and gave us a three-page spread with photos.

I remember one night we'd finished gigging early and had all returned to the hotel. Joan had joined the tour that day. It was only eleven or so, neither of us was tired, and we were in a mischievous mood. Bobby Colomby's room was across the hall, so I walked across and listened at his door. He was sweet-talking a young lady in his inimitable fashion, and I silently laughed as I took in his secret persuasions. After awhile, it became quiet. I gave them about ten minutes to develop their new relationship before bludgeoning Bob's door.

"Who's there?"

"Police. Open up in there!" I imitated, as Joan strolled across the hall with my Polaroid.

"Just a minute," Bobby stalled, to the sounds of intense rustling from inside his room. Finally, the door opened and Bobby appeared in his shirt, with one leg in his pants and two out. FLASH! went the Polaroid. Hysterical went Joan and me as we collapsed laughing in the hallway.

Bobby took it pretty well until I regained my composure and recited his seduction rap of the past hour verbatim. Red-faced, he pulled me into the bathroom.

"This is the only way I can show you how embarrassed I am," he said, plunging his naked foot completely into the toilet and flushing it continuously.

After he regained his composure, he decided it was a great joke, and shouldn't we try it on Steve? This time Bobby would call ahead to Steve's room and warn him that the police were ransacking everyone's room. Then I would hammer on his door. Give it a little more credibility.

Bobby on the phone: "Steve? I'm glad I got you. I can't really talk much but the cops are going through everyone's room, and they've got search warrants and they're being really vicious and I don't—"

BAM BAM BAM!

Steve on the phone: "Omygod they're here, gotta go!"

Steve must have been *truly* terrified, because he was rooming with one of the horn players who was by far the biggest doper in the band. He must have flushed half of Mexico down the toilet in about three seconds. He then came to the door, opened it and FLASH! I have another shot for my growing Polaroid collection. This time I'm in tears I'm laughing so hard, crawling down the hallway, leaving Steve talking to the wall: "That's the meanest shit I've ever seen. . . ."

Flushed with our success, we sorted out the vulnerable ones in the band for our caper, and all of them got their picture taken that night. If the Polaroids hadn't faded, they would have made a great album cover.

Just to balance out the karma, the band repaid me the next day. We were flying from Boston to Chicago, and the group was

Mr. and Mrs. Samuel Kooper are proud to announce the marriage of their son Alan to a Fender Telecaster covered with decals; February, 1968, at Winterland. PHOTO: JIM MARSHALL.

massed at the gate a half hour before departure time. I was sitting there in the cheap fur coat I had bought for the winter and this weird moustache I had grown for the tour. The stares were a little heavier than usual, it being proper Boston and all. Bobby came over with his carry-on bag and asked me if I'd watch if for him while he went to the magazine stand. Sure. Then Steve with the same request. Pretty soon I was surrounded by everyone's luggage, all by myself in this stupid coat and moustache, and everyone walking by was breaking up that this weird looking asshole is travelling with twenty-seven pieces of luggage. They were *even* with me.

In St. Louis, we had to cancel the gig 'cause I had lost my voice, and Columbia wanted me in shape for the more important San Francisco and L.A. dates. We signed some autographs at the place we were supposed to play and made it back to the hotel. Don Johnston, our roadie, Jerry Weiss, and I were in my room, spacing out on how boring St. Louis was at 11:00 P.M. on Tuesday night.

"Let's escape!" I suggested. "We're gonna fly to Frisco in the morning, so why don't we just fly out tonight and not tell anyone."

We called the airport and, sure enough, there was a 2:45 nonstop with three empty seats calling our names. We packed our shit and snuck out without anyone in the band seeing us. A definite caper.

There was only one other passenger on the flight, an old lady in first class. The stewardesses turned out to be hip and not at all hard to look at. It was not long before we were getting high and necking. It was surrealistic. These things do not happen on commercial flights.

We landed in Frisco about 5:45 A.M. and deplaned, concealing about half the equipment, cargo, and miniature booze bottles they had on board, courtesy of our new "girlfriends." The prize possession was the battery-operated emergency bullhorn, which Don Johnston won from his fair damsel (this was later to get us nearly kicked out of our hotel for disturbing the other occupants by calling the band to quarters at 4:00 A.M.).

While we were waiting for our real luggage, Jerry Weiss was leaning against the wall trying to adjust to his new life-style. Quite a difference from pushing up a horn in the back row of Larry Elgart's dance band. Jerry just kept saying over and over, "It didn't happen. I can't believe it!"

The bags came and we jumped in a taxi and headed for the hotel. No sooner did we pull away from the curb than the driver turns around and asks if "anyone wants to get high." That was it for Jerry. New Yorkers aren't used to such mellowness, especially in the traditional armored attack vehicle known as the taxi. He didn't ever wanna leave California.

Back in St. Louis, meanwhile, "the great escape" had been easily ascertained. Noting the absence of our luggage, no one was uptight; they knew we were in California. But they sho' was jealous when they got there and heard about our pie-in-the-sky!

•

We returned from the tour with a developing reputation and an album entering the charts. It was decided that we needed to tighten up, so we took up residence at the Garrick Theater (adjoining the Cafe Au GoGo) following the Mothers, who had concluded a *six-month* stint there. I was hoping we wouldn't stay quite so long. The Mothers moved downstairs to the GoGo, and the Electric Flag moved in across the street at the Bitter End. BB King arrived to open at the Generation Club, and you'd best believe the Village was jumpin'. In between sets we would catch the Mothers, along with the Flag, who had the same schedule we did. We weren't able to catch their show and vice versa.

When our last show ended, however, BB King's started. We used to finish up and catch the tail end of his set. I sat in his dressing room after the show, renewing a friendship with one of the most sincere, incredible human beings to ever set foot on the planet. I told him about the new band, and we figured out that his schedule made it hard for him to catch us. He was real interested in hearing us, though. I put on my thinking cap.

The next night when BB finished his last set, BS&T was in the audience. They closed the club doors and we hopped onstage to play an after-hours set for BB and the employees of Generation.

We played about forty-five minutes and before our closer began, I invited BB to join us on it. It was "Somethin' Goin' On," a tune I'd written in the style of BB King. We played up to the guitar solo and then dropped the volume way down and BB played, building slowly to his inevitable climax. As the horns eased in behind him, he took a step forward and *really* began to play. Obviously inspired, he played things I had never heard him or any other guitar player play before. He was rocking from side to side smiling, and as each verse ended, I yelled out, "Don't stop now, Bee," and he was up and away again. After ten minutes he took it down, and the band and the audience went nuts. Even if we had had the foresight to record it, I don't think anyone would've believed it. Elvin Bishop was in the audience and he later concurred that, indeed, it was the best he remembered ever hearing BB play. It was ten minutes of sheer ecstasy I will never forget.

The seeds of discontent had been sown, and it was only a matter of time before they blossomed. In the Blues Project, we had done everything together. Knowing such behavior did not solidify group unity, I attempted the opposite with BS&T. I only hung with the band at rehearsals or gigs, preferring the confines of home and the company of wife Number 2 (Al finally marries Joan at City Hall). The formation of the band had a stabilizing effect on my previous mental aberrations, and my subsequent abandonment of drugs made me the straightest one in the band (although certainly not the straightest looking).

I thought all this would improve my relationship with the various members of the band, hopefully delaying overkill for at least a year. But while I was busy keeping to myself, the band was forming into various little political pockets (the Colomby-Katz faction most notably), and musical revolution was in the air. The failure of my voice to endure on the tour had caused concern and unbeknownst to yours truly, plans were afoot to change all that.

One of my concepts was that Freddie and I would write an arrangement, and the band was required to play it in its entirety *one* time to my satisfaction before any suggestions were offered. At that point I could take suggestions, and usually did. I will admit I ran my dream a *little* Hitleresque, but I was trying to prevent it from becoming a nightmare. (Witness Jeff Lynne and ELO.)

The beginning of the end came at rehearsal one day. Freddie and I had written an arrangement of Stevie Winwood's "Dear Mr. Fantasy," to be played for the first time that day. I double-checked the parts as I handed them out and was surprised to find they had been altered from what Freddie and I had arranged. Bobby had taken the liberty to go over to Freddie's and change the parts around without bothering to ask anyone. Freddie, quiet sweetheart that he is, was easy to manipulate toward this end.

The Beast and the Beauty; me and Joanie, '67. PHOTO: PETER HUJAR.

Freddie and I had spent at least four hours on that arrangement, but our work had been erased and there was no way we would be able to hear it.

I walked out of rehearsal. I suppose Bobby was trying to show me what life was like under *my* rule, but I didn't get the hint. Also, I couldn't help thinking back to the day we decided to form the band. My contingency for going along with it was that it would be under my guidance and leadership, and everyone readily agreed.

I suppose the final spark that incited the mutiny was my growing dissatisfaction with Steve's progress as a player. He was, at best, adequate, and I felt he was holding the band back from some incredible musical pyrotechnics. I went around to each member separately and suggested that Steve be replaced. To a man I was turned down cold. Of course, I wasn't aware that *my* offing was in the cards, and I assumed they didn't want to upset the delicate balance that was holding the band together. So I could keep basically honest, I approached Steve and told him what I had done. Instead of calmly taking it in, or as a rather crude instructional criticism of his playing, he went nuts.

The next day a band meeting was held at our lawyer's, who happened to be Steve's brother: nepotism I was too blind to notice. Before we could even come to verbal blows, Randy took the floor and announced he had been offered the trumpet chair in Horace Silver's group, and he thought he was gonna take it. Bobby freaked out and filibustered in an attempt to talk him out of it. Randy's loss to the band would be a heavy one. Even so, I defended his position on a growth basis. Horace had never hired a white man in his group before, and so Randy would be participating in history. What an honor. Horace had been one of my boyhood idols, and I also knew Randy would be happier with the freedom of expression he could find in that situation. Randy was a genius player, but you can't force a man one way when his mind is made up the other. Bobby sat down exasperated. There were cracks in his ship even *he* hadn't anticipated.

Then the shit hit the band. Bobby said he felt we should hire a lead singer due to my limited capabilities and my lack of tour

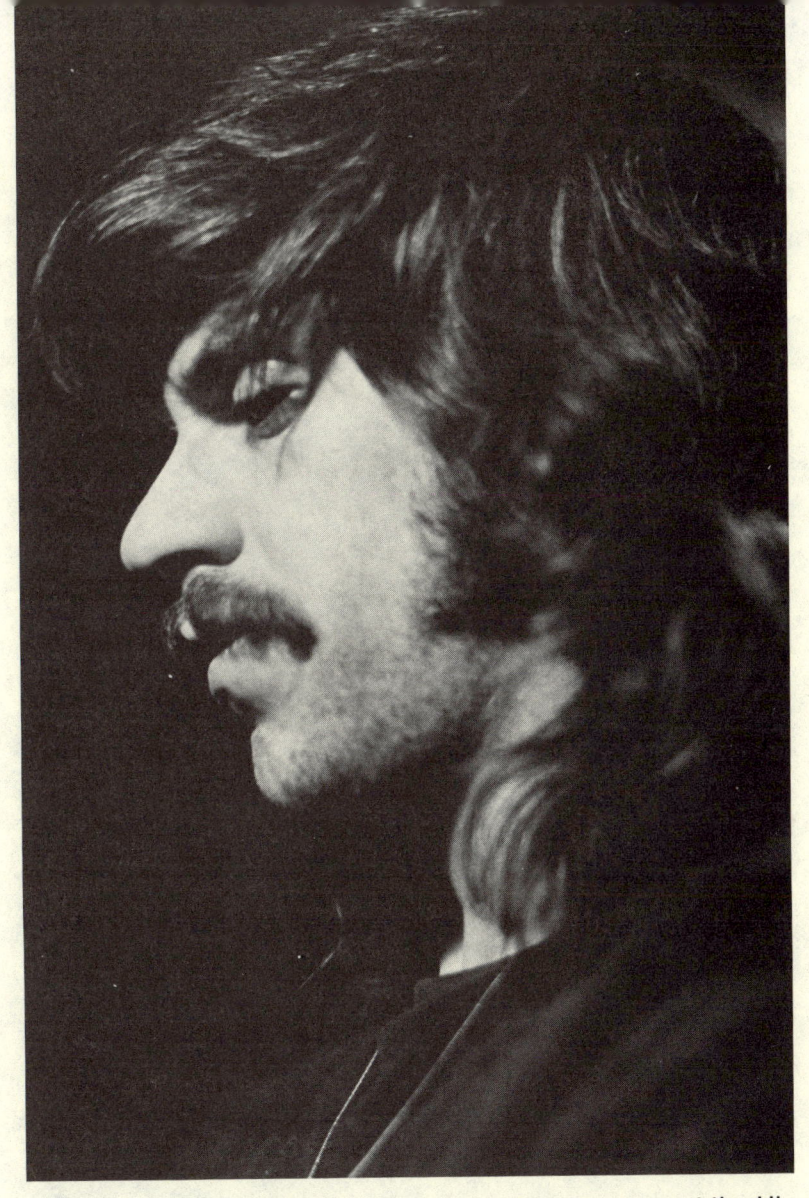

Freddie Lipsius after graduating from his crash course at the Hip Institute. PHOTO: ALICE OCHS.

endurance, and I should be relegated to organist and composer/arranger. He was totally prepared in his support. I was certainly aware I was not one of rock's trendsetting vocalists, but I was at least as good at what I did as Steve was at what he did. But I guess they wanted a new singer more than I wanted a new guitarist. There were tears in my eyes as I left the meeting, 'cause I knew the dream was over.

David Clayton-Thomas finds out he's been accepted into Blood Sweat & Tears. PHOTO: ALICE OCHS.

It was heavy drama at the Garrick that night. All of us knew it was over, but we didn't know when it was gonna come to final blows. We played a tense first set, culminating in Jerry Weiss telling me, "Go fuck yourself," right in the middle of the encore. It knocked the air out of me. I called everyone into the dressing room.

"OK," I said, "you don't want me in the band, you don't want to play the tunes I choose, I don't want to bring you down. I'll go away and make my music somewhere else. Anybody who wants to join me is welcome, because you win—I quit. I'm sorry it had to end like this." And I was out the door.

As I rounded the corner, I heard Bobby saying; "Can't you see what he's trying to do . . ." and I realized that it would be impossible for me to be in a group again. Because simply, I wasn't trying to do *anything*. I had been defeated in an arena where I was at my acknowledged best, and with that I retired from participating in the world of bands.

I ran into Freddie in the men's room. He was real down and disillusioned. Said he was gonna go back to school. No, I said. Stay with 'em. They need you to hold the band together if it can, indeed, survive me and Randy splitting.

Freddie did stay on, and everyone knows the rest of the story. With David Clayton-Thomas to replace me as singer, and Dick Halligan to cover my organ playing, with half a new repertoire, and a new producer (James William Guercio), they went on to set trends and records in the music business. I was proud when their next album hit Number 1. Even though I lost all financial interest, *I* knew where it all began. God bless you, Maynard Ferguson.

What's wrong with this picture? The 1968 assembly of the A&R staff of Columbia Records at their annual sales convention in San Juan, Puerto Rico. Far right (in more ways than one): John Hammond, Sr., and Bugeyes Allie. PHOTO: COLUMBIA RECORDS.

7

Up against the Expense Account

The day after Jerry Weiss told me off on stage, I found myself in Clive Davis's office at Columbia Records, trying to explain to him the changes his $40,000-plus investment was putting itself through.

"Well, they don't like me, they don't want me to sing anymore. I mean what would you do? I quit and, uh, I really had no choice. It was like Profumos's resignation."

Clive suggested I stay with the band until a suitable replacement could be found. Concerned with my personal safety, I flatly dismissed any such notion (as I imagined they certainly would), and that brought me to the other reason for my visit that day.

"Clive, I've decided to produce records full-time now. I'm in no position to record a solo album or join (much less form) a band at this point. Being that you have me signed individually as an artist, I felt you should have first refusal on my services as a producer. Let me know what you think within a week."

He was still wondering about his investment as I bade my bye-byes out the door.

Four days later Walter Dean, head of CBS business affairs, called to say that I had a job. I was bouncing off the peeling walls of my ghetto palace with joy. Columbia had called my bluff, but I was (sort of) ready to deliver. I felt this was an important decision on Clive's part for two reasons: 1) I was sure there would be other people with plights similar to mine in the near future and, if my test run proved successful, perhaps large companies would open their doors to them. And, 2) It was something of a precedent for a major corporation at that time to *hire* a freak on staff.

BE: The concept of a company freak did not originate with Al. It's a proud tradition which can be traced back to pioneers Billy James at Columbia and Danny Fields at Elektra, company men whose hearts were with the music and the artists. Al was the first established rock musician to voluntarily scale the fence of the corporate playground, and the following years have seen his lead followed by Jim Messina, Spencer Davis, and others, although they were not actually on staff as Al was.

A contract was to be signed and, being that I had no manager, I wound up representing myself. To a hippie busting his guts to hold down $150 a week, double that amount, an expense account, an office, and a secretary seemed like moving next door to Howard Hughes. Later I found out that they got me for comparative peanuts, but for the time being I was in nirvana. I moved my wife and other belongings to a rat-free apartment house on the edge of the Village (which also, ironically, housed one-time Blues Project manager Sid Bernstein, Au GoGo magnate Howard Solomon, and Verve Folkways' Prez Jerry Schoenbaum. Talk about living in your past). I bought some new clothes, got a haircut, and began the next phase of Allie in Wonderland.

•

I sat in my office the first day and just beamed. My secretary had previously worked for some guy who recorded original cast albums for Broadways shows, and she was downright terrified of me. I didn't know what was going on in this weird-ass building, and she certainly wasn't gonna go out of her way to clue me in. Next door to me was an old friend named Wally Gold, who'd been Aaron Schroeder's assistant throughout my writing career,

Up Against the Expense Account | 183

also just starting work there. That was reassuring. Wally, however, was their easy listening great white hope, and was soon devilishly busy producing Peter Nero, Jerry Vale, and Barbra Streisand.

On my right was the office of John Hammond, Sr., who is a certifiable legend in his own time, having discovered Dylan, Billie Holiday, Aretha Franklin, and Bruce Springsteen all in the same career. His son, John, Jr., was an established blues singer and a good buddy of mine, and it was easy for his pop and me to establish a rapport. John was a sly guy. He kept to himself so folks weren't sure *what* the ole gent was ever up to, but he knew what he liked and he never lost his ears. He had no use for business by the books, which used to freak people out up there, but *I* could relate to that. In essence, he was the original Columbia Records hippie.

Across the hall from me was David Rubinson, who produced most of the underground albums recorded by staff producers. I found out later he was instrumental in getting me hired, and I owe a debt to him for that. David produced Moby Grape, the Chambers Brothers, Taj Mahal, Tim Rose, and an avant-garde group called the United States of America. I first met him when I sat in on the Moby Grape *Wow Grape Jam* album (the *real* first rock jam-session album). David has since realized the promise he showed then by producing and managing some of the finest acts on the scene today, including Herbie Hancock and the Pointer Sisters.

The interior of the floor I worked on was Fellini-ish. It was designed by some guy who had probably always dreamed of doing European doctors' offices but got stuck with a record company in New York instead. This development evidently didn't deter him. The color scheme was your basic chiaroscuro (black and white); could wear a referee's shirt to work and blend right in with the environment. The part that killed me was that the walls to each office were prefab (and that don't mean *before fabulous*) and the more important you got, the wider your office suddenly became. I had your medium-sized shot, an uncommonly lucky debut. One guy in Artist Relations (I *still* don't know what that means) had the tiniest office, barely large enough to accommodate a desk and two chairs. He had to beg use of someone else's office if he had a meeting with more than one person.

You were not allowed to bring your own wall hangings to your office; framed paintings of someone's choice had arrived long before you did. They were permanently fastened to the prefab walls, so you couldn't adjust their position, or swap 'em like baseball cards. I had a pretty groovy George Gershwin portrait, so I didn't mind.

Oh, I mustn't forget my plant. I inherited a plant; medium sized, good vibes, and all that. Every day at 6:15 P.M., some nondescript guy would come around and water everyone's plants. I mean, he wouldn't care for them or even look at them for that matter, just pour the prescribed amount of H_2O in the bucket, yawn, and stumble on to the next one.

The eleventh floor housed the pop A&R staff, the studio, booking department, the classical department, and the exec offices (relative lower echelon). Davis and Walter Dean were here, but the biggies, Paley and Stanton and Leiberson, were somewhere else. The only time I ever saw Leiberson was at the annual conventions, where he would circulate quite a bit and display an engaging sense of humor. He was well liked.

After the first week of staring around, meeting everyone and getting a new secretary, it was time to get down to business. The problem was that there was *none* to get down to. I hadn't found or discovered any great bands, I wasn't ready to make a solo album, and nobody from the company suggested I cut any acts that were already signed to the label. I was full of piss and vinegar; I was ready to *produce* someone, something, the plant in my office, anything, I didn't give a shit. Just cut me loose in that studio!

I was also aware of the fact that I didn't have any up-to-date experience in that particular area, although I watched John Simon like a hawk as he produced that first BS&T album. My influences were most notably Simon, Phil Spector (king of sixties producers in sound innovation), and George Martin. But having the taste in the records I listened to didn't necessarily qualify me to make them.

One day, an absurdly simple solution popped into my cranium.

Why not just get a bunch of proven players in the studio and fuck around? CBS would pay for it (hopefully) and I could finish up my post-grad record producing course. Maybe it would sell enough to pay for itself. I decided to call Mike Bloomfield in San Francisco and find out what he was doing.

•

There had been an amazing parallel between Mike Bloomfield's career and mine. We both came into the public eye from our appearance on Dylan's *Highway 61* album (where we met). We both served apprenticeships in pioneer electric blues bands (Paul Butterfield/Blues Project). We both started relatively avant-garde horn bands of our own (Electric Flag/BS&T) and eventually got kicked out of them.

I got him on the phone and it turned out he was not doing much of anything. "Why don't we just go in the studio," I proposed, "and just fuck around and jam. Columbia'll put it out and big deal."

"Okay," he says, "just let's do it in California." We picked the sidemen (I chose bassist Harvey Brooks, my boyhood buddy late of The Flag; Bloomers chose Eddie Hoh, The Mamas and the Papas' drummer, known as Fast Eddie) and set the dates.

To make sure everyone was comfy, I commandeered a house in L.A. It was a nifty job with a pool that fellow producer David Rubinson had been using while cutting Taj Mahal. It had two weeks to run on his month, and it seemed like a drag to just waste it. I got there a few days early and swam my New York ass off 'til Harvey and Bloomfield hit town.

Michael always has some *problem* which he carries around with him; it's like a cross he enjoys bearing (part of his American-Jewish heritage). This time around he arrived with an ingrown toenail which he kept insisting was gangrene. As soon as he walked in, he took one of the expensive crystal bowls from the kitchen and soaked his big toe in it for an hour. His injured toe is immortalized on the back of the album for all you blues purists.

That night we hit the studio and got right down to business. Barry Goldberg, also late of the Flag, came down and sat in on a few tracks. We recorded a slow shuffle, a Curtis Mayfield song, a Jerry Ragavoy tune, a real slow blues, a three-quarter modal jazz-type tune, and in nine hours had half an album in the can.

Jim Marshall and Linda Ronstadt came down to visit, and Jim snapped away on his Nikon, documenting that evening on film. There was a real comfortable feeling to the proceedings, and while listening to one of the playbacks I noted that I had gotten the best recorded Bloomfield ever and, after all, that was the whole point of the album. We piled in the rent-a-car and made it back to "Big Stink" (as we called the house, after Michael's toe), crashing mightily with dreams of finishing the album the next night.

What happened next is one of those quirks of fate that you can't explain, but you never question in retrospect. The phone starts jangling at 9:00 A.M. and it's some friend of Bloomfield's, asking if he'd made the plane 'cause she was waiting at the airport to pick him up.

"Huh? Michael's fast asleep in the next—hold on," I said, doing an O. J. Simpson outta bed into the next bedroom to find . . . an envelope? And, inside, "Dear Alan. Couldn't sleep well . . . went home . . . sorry."

Shit! Race back to the phone. Nobody there. I got half an album, studio time and musicians booked, and the turkey can't sleep in the $750 a month dungeon with the heated pool. My first corporate hassle. ("Well, Clive, of course I'm aware of the costs, but he couldn't sleep. I mean, haven't you ever had insomnia?" No way *that* was gonna work.)

It's 9:15 in the morning and my mind and ulcers are havin' a foot race for the finish line. I'm actually on the verge of packin' it in myself, but a cooler part of my head prevailed. I methodically

Recording *Super Session:* Alan and Michael. PHOTO: JIM MARSHALL.

"I didn't even consider people would find this boring." A tense moment in the studio. PHOTO: JIM MARSHALL.

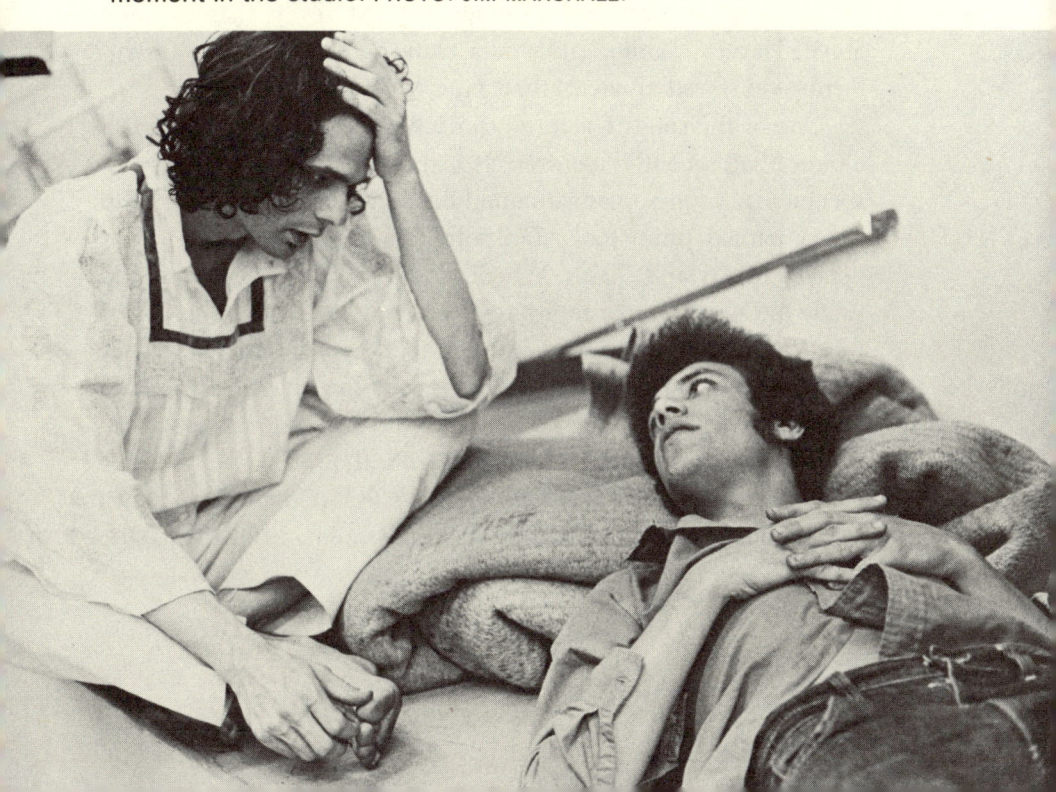

made out a list of all the guitar players I dug who lived on the West Coast. At noon I started callin' 'em—Randy California, Steve Miller, Steve Stills, Jerry Garcia. By 5:00 I had a confirm on one player and left it at that. Once again, good ol' fate stepped in to save my ass in the person of Steve Stills, also unemployed by the breakup of *his* band, The Buffalo Springfield.

Steve was primarily known as a singer-songwriter, and mainly on the West Coast, but I knew he was a hot guitar player and was more than willing to give him a try. (Besides I had no choice, did I?) At 5:00 I tried Ahmet Ertegun in New York, but it was three hours later there and Atlantic Records was closed for the day. Steve was signed to Atlantic, and you just don't make records for other labels without permission; another corporate hassle. Steve was one of my favorite singers and to have his voice on the album would've upgraded it 200 percent, but at that point I felt it would've endangered the release of the album by tying up Atlantic and Columbia in one of those red tape battles that pencil pushers are so fond of. It's bad enough he's gonna *play* without permission, I thought; let's leave it at that and cross our fingers, hoping Atlantic will let us use *his* fingers. Steve had just gotten his first stack of Marshall amps and was chompin' at the bit to blast his Les Paul through 'em. At seven that evening Steve, Harvey, Eddie, and yours truly sat down at our instruments and stared at each other. Now what?

One of the songs I wanted to do was inspired by an English album I had recently acquired. It featured the performances of a spectacular young organist named Brian Auger and a trendy mod singer named Julie (Jools) Driscoll. The album contained their version of Dylan's "This Wheel's on Fire," which was a top single in Europe, and a rambling version of Donovan's "Season of the Witch." I thought it would be nice for us to do it, 'cause it provided a lot of room for improvisation and everyone already had the basics of the song down. We did two takes straight off, and the version we kept was edited from the two.

When I played on *Highway 61 Revisited* we'd cut some songs two or three times with different arrangements each time. One

The gentle grizzly bear watches the funky cowboy address the neo-foppish producer: Harvey Brooks, Steve Stills, and I talk during the recording of *Super Session*. PHOTO: JIM MARSHALL.

such song was "It Takes a Lot to Laugh, It Takes a Train to Cry." We originally recorded it as a fast tune, but Dylan opted for a slower version cut a few days later as the keeper for his album. I pulled out the fast version and taught it to everyone and we had song number two.

A staple number in Buddy Guy and Junior Well's repertoire was Willie Cobb's "You Don't Love Me." It's usually done as a shuffle, but I found it lent itself well to a heavy-metal eighth note feel. Later, when I mixed the album, I put the two-track mix through a process called *phasing* that gave it an eerie jet-plane effect.

It was 3:00 A.M. and we had three tunes under our belt, leaving us one or two tunes short of an album side. We racked our brains but to no avail. Then Harvey said he had just written a tune that we might like, and played it for us on the guitar. We did and that became the final tune on the album. It was called "Harvey's Tune" at that time, but was later included with a lyric on an Electric Flag album as "My Woman Who Hangs around the House." *Nice title, Harvey.*

I left for New York a day later with the tapes and continued working on the album there. I put on all my vocals, added some horns for variety, and mixed it slowly and deliberately. After all, this was my debut as a producer, and I wanted it to be as competent as possible. I played it for the big boys at CBS and they thought it was OK enough to release. Bruce Lundvall, a kindly V.P. (currently president of Columbia Records) baptized the collection *"Super Session."* Six weeks later, they unleashed it on the market.

Fully aware that this was just a furthering of the *Grape Jam* concept, and considering the relative infamy of Bloomfield, Stills, and myself, I didn't delude myself that this was going straight up to Number 1 or anything. It was merely something for me to do while I learned a new craft. I was back in L.A. the day it hit the stores, and ambled into one to see the initial reaction. I swear they were sailin' 'em over the counter like Beatle records fer chrissake!

In a matter of weeks it was Top Twenty and finally peaked at eleven. But that was plenty. This was a first for me. It only cost $13,000 to make, and soon it was a gold album (for sales exceeding 450,000). I found this particularly ironic. All my life I'd broken my ass to make hit records. Now me and these two other schmucks go in the studio for two nights, don't really give a shit, and boom, a best-seller.

In retrospect, I think that's what sold the record. The fact that, for the first time in any of our careers, we had nothing at stake artistically. Also, we had brought another ounce of respectability to rock 'n' roll by selling a jam session as "serious" music, something that had only been done in jazz circles up 'til then. All of a sudden, I had the respect of the CBS shorthairs. Shortly thereafter, due to the tremendous success of Blood, Sweat & Tears' second album, my BS&T album turned to gold, and then there were two (gold albums that is).

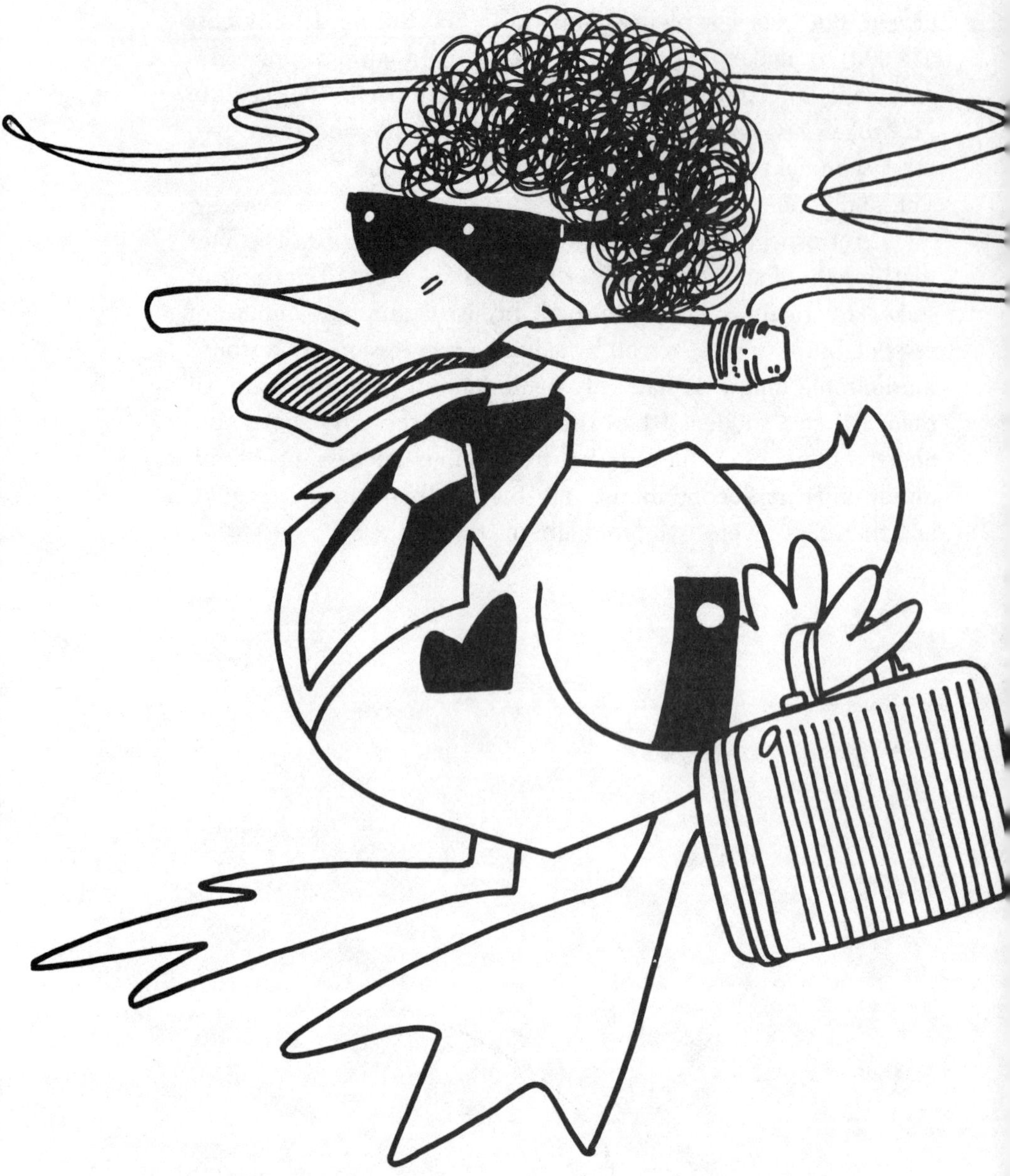

8

I Stand Accused and Other Adventures: A Tale of Two Albums

With *Super Session's* success, things became a lot more comfortable around the corporate towers. Instead of being the company freak, I was the company-freak-with-the-number-eleven-LP-on-the-charts, an important distinction. I had already been through three secretaries (who quit or asked to be transferred) and still didn't understand the ramifications of the "paperwork system."

The first single I produced at CBS was by Tim Rose, an artist I inherited from David Rubinson. David had previously cut some great sides with him ("Hey, Joe" and "Morning Dew," real big in England, where Jeff Beck and Jimi Hendrix copied Tim's versions and outsold him). For this project, I picked one of Tim's new songs and gave him one I chose from my record collection. It was a little-known song by a Canadian group, the Collectors, called "Looking at a Baby." Tim's song was called "Long Haired Boy."

We decided to use horns and strings on it, and it was necessary to engage the services of an arranger. I hired Charlie Calello, who had arranged all The Four Seasons' big hits, and had arranged and produced Laura Nyro's fine album *Eli and the 13th Confession*. I taught Tim the Collectors' song and fluently learned his song, and Calello and I sat down to write the arrangements. It was love at first note; and Charlie and I had a tremendous musical affinity. We respected each other, and the exchange of ideas was refreshing for both of us.

Anyway, we created this really avant-garde single with phasing and echo-plex repeating bassdrums, and Tim's song came out as the A side. I mixed the single and sent the tapes in to my superiors. A week after I expected it to be out, I strolled down the hall to the guy's office who was in charge of single releases. "Got any copies of my Tim Rose single?" I asked.

"Nope," he said.

When might you, I ask.

He consults his files. "Al, did you ever file a singles release requisition form?"

"File one," I said, "what the fuck *is* one?"

Needless to say, after much painful paper work, a month later my Tim Rose single came out. I imagine it is now a collectors' item of the highest order. I saw Tim recently, and *he* didn't even have one!

With *Super Session* making its way down the charts and my Tim Rose single in the toilet, I needed some product on the street. I got a bad case of bandwagon fever (**BE: An old record business adage which advises that if it's a hit, do it to death**) and decided to cut a followup to the *Super Session* album. One of the only criticisms of that LP was that it was a studio album and therefore, uninspired. Always one to want to shove it up a critic's ass, I decided to cut a live jam album, possibly at the Filmore. I called Bloomfield and he said sure, I owe you one (for when he snuck out of the other album).

This time he chose his friend and neighbor, John Kahn, on bass, and I selected Skip Prokop, who had just quit a Canadian group I was friendly with, The Paupers, on drums. I couldn't get Steve Stills this time due to prior commitments on his part, and mostly on instruction from my higher-ups, who evidently were still embroiled in the legal aspects of our last venture.

I called Bill Graham and asked if he would book us in for a weekend, and could we record it? He said sure. We scheduled it

Charlie Calello terrifies photographer while protecting Kooper, who is engaged in picking yet another hit. PHOTO: SANDY SPEISER, CBS.

about five weeks in advance, and I began making arrangements. I figured on ten days of rehearsal in Marin County, where Michael lived. I booked Wally Heider's remote truck to record the proceedings, got a budget OK, and things were lookin' good. Skip arrived from Toronto, and we were scheduled to begin rehearsing the next day.

I left rehearsal arrangements up to Bloomfield, 'cause it was his home turf and he had all the grease in town. He booked us into this strange place called the Mill Valley Heliport. Actually, it's the upstairs to the waiting room and repair shop of the heliport. For some reason, bands had been renting out the top floor and rehearsing there for quite a few years.

When we arrived, we found the band that had loaned us their room and equipment had got a last minute gig out of town, and the place was padlocked. Peering through a crack in the door, I noticed that the lion's share of their equipment was gone as well, so efforts to obtain a key were abandoned. After a few frantic phone calls by Michael, we piled into the rent-a-wagon and drove thirty-five miles into the woods to a house owned by a friendly bunch of freaks who called themselves the Anonymous Artists of America. They were a band that played "avant-garde poetic music" and featured a topless female bass player named Trixie Merkin. They had just returned from a weekend's work (can you imagine where?), and we all pitched in unloading their equipment to facilitate the beginnings of a first rehearsal.

Soon we were jamming away, and the combination of musicians seemed to work very nicely, considering we had never played together before. Everything went real smoothly but, at the end of the second day's rehearsal, we were pleasantly evicted in deference to *their* rehearsals. I was starting to sweat it, but Rock Scully, The Grateful Dead's manager, lent us their place for three days.

All of a sudden it was Thursday, and we were to open that night. We were half ready. We had six tight worked-out tunes and about ten frameworks for jam situation. The last three days of rehearsal Michael's famed insomnia returned, and he had not

A Tale of Two Albums | 197

slept at all in that time. He was reeling around the dressing room, and I couldn't believe he was gonna get up there and remember all these songs and play his ass off like me and Columbia Records were counting on him to do. Well, here goes.

We mount the stage (**AK: Show business is so sexual**) and tune up. Just as Bill Graham is about to introduce us, Michael grabs the mike and delivers his own introduction (and I quote): "Uhhh . . . listen here now, here's the thing of this gig and here's . . . I'll tell you about it now. Uh, awhile ago my friend Alan Kooper (**AK: It always struck me weird that Bloomfield always referred to me as Alan, and I referred to him as Michael, as we were commonly known as Mike and Al**) called me on the phone and said, 'Let's make this gig, an LP in Los Angeles, and we'll jam together and we'll see what will happen!' So we went and I played, and I played one day in the studio with Alan and I went back to San Francisco where I live (**AK: Very good, Michael**) and the other day Stephen Stills played . . . and they put out an

Two Jews' blues. Al: You realize, if we do this again in six months, in front of a live audience, we can make twice as much money. Mike: (expression says it all). PHOTO: JIM MARSHALL.

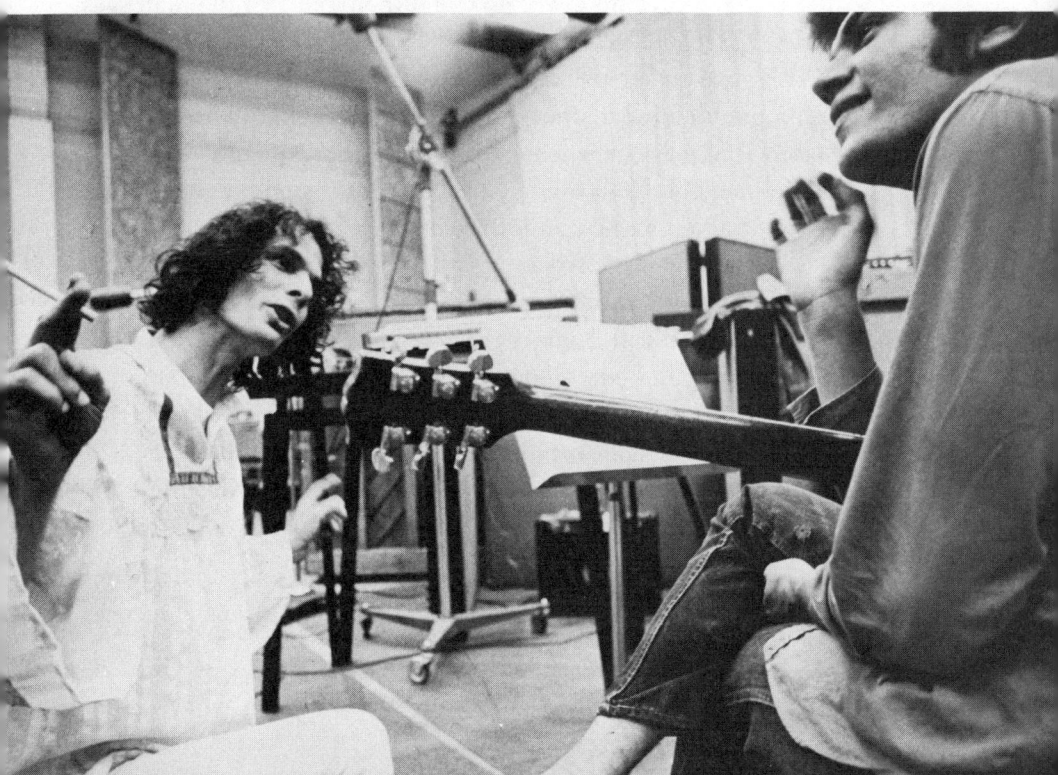

album called *Super Session* (**AK: I wish it had been that easy**). And then Alan said, OK, that's a groovy thing, let's play a super session, you know, let's do a session and play somewhere! (**AK: Yeah, those were my exact words.**) So I said, Awright man! Now this is exactly what's gone into this thing, I'll tell ya about it now . . .

"Now we played together once on the LP session, that was the one time, and then we practiced together the three days, the four of us: that's John Kahn, and Skip Prokop, and Alan. Now, I've jammed with John a few times, never with Skip. Alan, I guess, has played with Skip, never with John (**AK: Okay, now you guess—who fucked the boss's daughter?**). And altogether we've played four days and so it's half a session, you know, half a session because we're gonna jam because WHAT THE HELL HOW MUCH DO WE KNOW, and the other half is numbers. But I want you to know this is the truth of where we're playing. See? Now you know where it's at . . . OK!" (**AK: If Bloomfield wrote Nixon's speeches, he'd still be president today.**)

That little monologue reduced me to gales of laughter, and I relaxed and played a real comfortable set. Everyone in the band was calm, and it worked. This is not to say that we didn't make mistakes and fuck up every now and then, but like the man says, WHAT THE HELL HOW MUCH DO WE KNOW, and after all, it's nice to let people know you're human beings and not preprogrammed machines vomiting out somebody else's music. Right? That was our whole concept. We were an antiband band. We felt anybody had the right to play with anybody for as long as they wanted to, no commitments, no image, just music.

Anyway, the first two nights go smoothly enough and I've got roughly enough material for an album already. The third morning I get a call from Michael's wife, Susie, saying that "he's in the hospital being sedated to sleep, he couldn't stand it anymore" (I presume she was talking about not sleeping as opposed to the gig). Well, he'd done it again.

So I moseyed on down to the Filmore office to tell Uncle Bill Graham the good news. I think I'd rather cut my dick off than

Backstage at the Fillmore with Jerry Garcia, Jack Casady, and a girl and guy I don't seem to recognize. PHOTO: JIM MARSHALL.

tell Bill Graham half his show ain't gonna make it that night. As expected, he went nuts, screaming as if I'd murdered his best friend. What the fuck do you want from me, I respond. I'm not in the fucking hospital! I'm in your office at *noon* offering to call everyone in town and you're chastising me. I'm here ready to play. And the other guy ain't runnin' out on your contract. It's just that he hasn't slept in a week.

All Bill knew was that it said Mike Bloomfield on the poster, and Mike Bloomfield wasn't gonna be there. He called up Michael's house and started screaming at Susie; telling her how unprofessional her old man is. She just got back from taking Mike to the hospital, and she let go with a barrage that leveled him. He's screaming and she's screaming and ... sometimes I hate show business.

I got on the phone and called Carlos Santana (a local hero not known outside San Francisco at the time), Elvin Bishop, Steve Miller, Jerry Garcia, and others. Once again San Francisco responds, and every musician in town shows up and offers his/her services. It was a helluva show that night. Steve, Carlos, and Elvin all came up and did three or four songs apiece, and we ended playing way past closing time. The audience was happy. Graham was happy. Columbia Records was happy.

And I was *confused.* Should we include the playing of the "guest artists" on the album? I mean, it was the essence of the whole concept and it would certainly spice up the record. It would also make it a double album, however, which is not as nearly as marketable due to cost.

Somehow, I was able to convince CBS to release the album under their KGP prefix, which meant two records for only a dollar above the price of one. I think it was the first rock record they did it with. Also, they must have thought long and hard because they were narrowing their profit margin by cheapening a follow-up to a Top Twenty album. We were not able to get Capitol Records' permission to include Steve Miller's performances (he played great; I got tapes of it in my house), but Elektra gave us permission to use Elvin Bishop's stuff, and

Carlos, who was a year and a half from releasing his first album, was unsigned at the time and available to be included on the album.

BE: The label he eventually signed with was Columbia; merely coincidence?

I must tell you what kind of a guy Elvin Bishop is, because I love him dearly to this day. The track that is included on the album with him is sort of a contest between me, trying to end the song due to curfew, and Elvin, lost in some blues half-dream playing through at least five obvious endings. I thought it added a great touch to the record, and I even explained what was happening in the liner notes so folks could enjoy it.

Well, late one night after the album had been out a month, I ran into Elvin in a bar. "Hey, Kooper, how 'ya doing? By the way I hate you for putting that piece of shit out on your album. It's

The notorious Barry Imhoff, once owner of New York's Generation Club, finds himself holding Bill Graham's campaign poster while in an obvious trance. PHOTO: JIM MARSHALL.

terrible and embarrassing and [before I can reply] ah, fuck it! It's out anyway, nothin' we can do about, lemme buy ya a drink!" And off he goes laughing into the night.

Now that is a *mellow dude.*

•

After looking through twenty rolls of film shot at the gigs, I couldn't find anything suitable for a cover. We considered a shot that would be doctored up to look like me and Michael jumping off the Golden Gate Bridge, but that got tired *fast.*

One Sunday, I was lying in bed watching the New York Jets sock it to the Denver Broncos. All of a sudden it hits me. Norman Rockwell! Let's get Norman Rockwell to paint a portrait of me and Michael. Is that fucking beautiful or what? I raced for the phone and called Bob Cato, the CBS art director, at home. Is it possible, can it be done? He said maybe and he'd check it out first thing in the morning.

A week later Michael and I are sitting in the photo studio at CBS waiting for Normie to photograph us so's he can paint our portrait. In he strolls, right on time, and Bloomfield, a closet-Rockwell-groupie, just gushes all over him. As it turned out, Michael was wearing his brother's coat, found a pill in the pocket, and took it. It was STP (superacid) and he was gooning out all over Normie.

"Oh man, you're the best. You should come to San Francisco though, man, you would see such sights there to paint. You wouldn't believe it. People in robes in the street, mothers suckling their young, I tell you it's just like *Jerusalem,* Norman, so whaddaya think?"

Norman, who's listening intently, just puffs on his pipe and he is *together.* He takes our pictures and chats amiably with Michael, thanks everyone, and then as Chuck Berry once so aptly put it, is "gone like a cool breeze."

Two weeks later, after Michael had returned home to Marin, Norman sent me an invitation to his opening at a ritzy New York gallery. First one he'd had in years; I'm honored. Me and the missus dressed up in the finest rockstar regalia 1968 had to offer

A rare photo of the Norman Rockwell experience: a little-known power trio from Nutley, New Jersey, that made one album and was never heard from again. PHOTO: BOB CATO, CBS.

(satin pants, nehru shirt, 2,000 beaded necklaces, embroidered jackets with fur cuffs, etc.) and we make it down to the gallery.

Now, we were as out of place as Richard Pryor at a KKK convention. And these folks, well, they're not shy about looking down their noses as we peruse old Normie's canvases. (And I must say he's got an impressive bunch of art there, I don't care who says he's not cool or what, the man has *soul!*) Just when it's getting really uncomfortable, Normie and his *great* wife come flying in the door, and who does he come over and hug? Not the Vanderbilts or the Rockefellers or the Von Furstenbergs, but Mr. and Mrs. Yours Truly, which causes the black sheep of the party to become the *who-is-that* of the evening.

He yanked us off to the office, where he relaxed and said, "I hate this stuff, I can't wait to get back home. It's so nice to see you again, I'm glad you could find the time to attend." His wife was mostly silent but she had that Norman-is-a-dear-old-guy-isn't-he look on her face, and this lady was obviously in love like a bitch and God knows how long they'd been married. Did my heart good, I tell you. My last words to him that night were, "Paint me a little heavier, it'll make my parents happy."

The painting arrived at CBS seven weeks later (he was doing Nixon's portrait at the same time, and it threw him off schedule, not to mention point of reference) in a cheap-o frame with this note: "Here is *The Blues Singers*. These boys were the most interesting looking people I've ever painted. Thank you, Norman."

Well, except for Bertrand Russell, I think he was probably right. If you notice, my face is a little fuller than in real life. My parents were thrilled.

Shortly thereafter, Columbia released the double album set *The Live Adventures of Mike Bloomfield & Al Kooper* with the Rockwell portrait on the cover. Included within was a version of Paul Simon's "Feelin' Groovy" featuring Paul singing over-dubbed harmony with me on the third verse. Also included were an instrumental of The Band's "The Weight," Booker T.'s "Green Onions," Traffic's "Dear Mr. Fantasy," and the usual

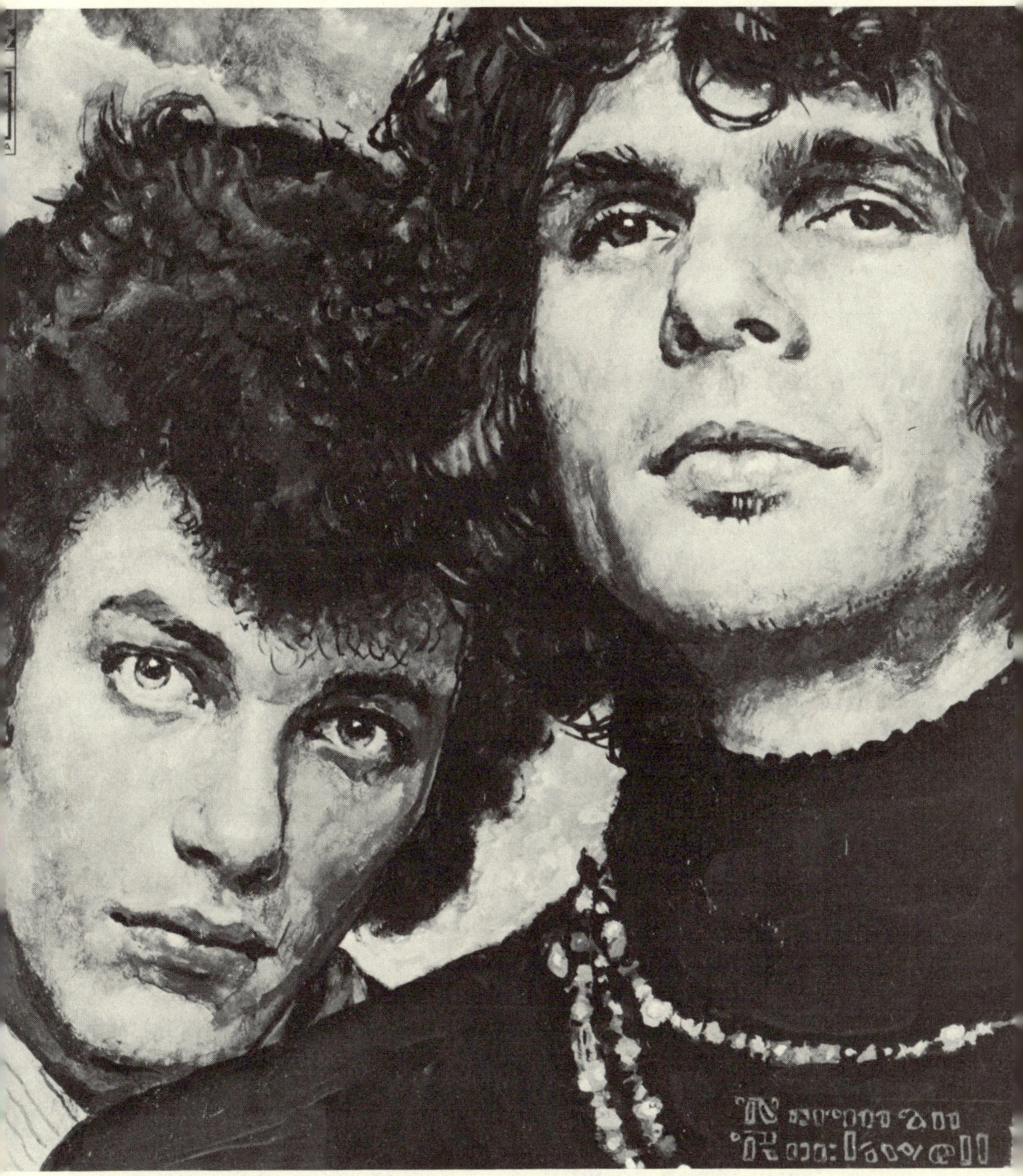

assortment of blues tunes. Guest appearances were credited to Carlos Santana (still unknown) and Elvin Bishop. The record made a handsome profit but never did duplicate the phenomenal success of *Super Session*. It covered me for awhile, though, as I finally began work on my first solo album.

•

The key factor was waiting out Blood, Sweat & Tears to see what tunes they were going to do so there was no duplication. From my original set, they kept "You Make Me So Very Happy," "Smiling Phases," "More & More," and the jam portion of "Somethin' Going On" called "Blues Part IV." I wrote some new tunes, chose a few others, and took one we had been doing with BS&T that they had opted not to record.

While I was working on other projects for Columbia, I did my album in the spare moments. I also experimented profusely by using Columbia's recording facilities in Nashville and Los Angeles as well as New York. In Nashville I was reunited with the *Blond on Blonde* band—Charlie McCoy, Charlie Daniels, Kenny Buttrey, Wayne Moss, and Jerry Kennedy, whom Bob Johnston was kind enough to assemble for me. I cut five tracks down there, six in New York, and one in Los Angeles.

I was producing an album on Don Ellis, the jazz trumpet player, and we wrote a chart together for his band to play on my new album. It was Stevie Winwood's "Colored Rain," and Don included instrumental sections in ⅞ time! When all the recording was finished, I assembled the album. When I got the right track order, I noticed that the differences between the different locations would be apparent to the listener, and some sort of bridge was necessary from track to track. I used a bunch of sound effects that were apropos to the tunes: a heart beating after a sad love song, a thunderstorm before "Colored Rain," and also a few left-field ones. At the beginning of Side Two, there is the extremely realistic sound of a police car complete with siren, driving closer and closer to the listener. Friends have told me over the years how they suffered tremendous paranoia from listening to it through earphones or having it on in the house as back-

Putting backgrounds on the *I Stand Alone* album with singers Maretha Stewart, Hilda Harris, and Eileen Gilbert. PHOTO: LLOYD ZIFF, CBS.

ground music. Some people were heading for the toilet with their stashes before they realized it was just the record! I included an overture (a holdover from the BS&T days) of sound effects as well as musical themes. The album was named after one of my new songs, "I Stand Alone." It seemed like a good title for my first solo album.

I didn't know what to do for the cover, so I dumped it in John Berg's lap. (He was the new art director for CBS following Bob Cato's departure, and he's still there today.) He came up with putting my face on the Statue of Liberty. I thought it would be hysterical to see this freak representing America, and made them add a shot of me up in the torch laughing just so everyone got the joke. On the back they got cartoonist Bill Charmatz to do a cartoon of me eating the Statue of Liberty (now don't rush out, it's not me eating her *carnally*). The inside was a photo collage, the track information, and a poem I had written when I was in the Blues Project that I felt explained why I was recording a solo album.

The album was released to mixed reviews, but a much more interesting phenomena took place at the same time. Coincidental with the release of the album, BS&T had thrown some quotes out in the press about why I had left the group, and I was depicted as some demonic egomaniac with whips and chains who kept them all in cages. Prior to all this, I really had no press image; I was neither black nor white, just a gray type of feller. When critics wrote about me there was no personality mentioned. It would say here's a good record by Al, or on this one Al turns in a mediocre performance, or just comments about the musicality of it all as opposed to the person himself. This was fine with me, 'cause that's all I was selling. I mean you can hate or enjoy my music, but me the person was really none of your business.

BE: Until now.

Somehow, probably because of BS&T's meteoric popularity and the release of my solo album, I got nailed with one of those real stinky press images. Then everything I had done was tied into the ego thing. People said when he says "I Stand Alone," he means there is no one comparable to him, that he's got an ego as big as the Statue of Liberty, etc. Reviews were taken up with this Rona Barrett shit instead of talking about the music.

This was the beginning of my interest in stepping permanently into the background. Fortunately, too, because my star was definitely on the wane. And so ended 1968.

PHOTO: MYRA ZELLER

9

Zoot Sims, Shuggie Otis, Don Ellis, a Manager, and the End of an Era

I guess I began the year 1969 planning on making a second solo album that would do me proud. I had been concentrating on my songwriting and had a fine crop of songs, diverse yet fairly commercial. I was putting it all together with Charlie Calello, the arranger with whom I'd worked on the Tim Rose single and my first solo album. We had become quite friendly by this time, and Charlie was privy to more and more of my business "dealings." Growing increasingly more horrified with my bungling of business affairs, one afternoon he could take it no more.

"You asshole," I believe were his exact words, "you should be earning ten times what you're taking in. Come sit down with my manager and see if he can do anything for you."

As ol' B. Dylan once said, when you ain't got nothin', you got nothin' to lose. The next day I'm sitting in my jeans and flowerpower in this distinguished guy's office. He's wearing a shirt and tie. That's the first manager I've seen in a shirt and tie in eight years. *What a square.*

He asked me what exactly I wanted out of all these records and shit. I thought for a minute and shot back, "A million bucks and the ability to retire when I'm thirty." And I wasn't kidding. That was my tangible goal.

Intangibly, I told him, I want to influence music in such a way that I can turn on the radio and hear exactly what I like as much of the time as possible. I had already accomplished this to a minor degree with *Super Session* and to a major degree with Blood, Sweat & Tears. But I wanted to do it at least once a year, in some form.

He listened attentively to all this, paused for a second, and said, "I can get you the million bucks. The retiring will be up to you, as will all the creative aspects of your career. I don't profess to know a goddam thing about what you do musically or creatively, but I can turn it into dollars in such a way that you will realize ten times what you are earning now in less than two years."

"What do I have to *do* to make all this money?" I asked almost hesitantly.

"Just do what you do and don't *ever* do business."

Now, after all, isn't this what every creative person dreams of? Someone to take the business hassles off their back so they can concentrate on their art exclusively? "What kind of contract are you looking for?" I asked, again hesitantly.

"No contract. When you think I'm doing the job you expect, you'll sign a contract if you want. It's the same contract that everyone else I manage signs."

The next night this guy comes to dinner at my house, with my present lawyer in attendance. Now up to this point, my lawyer was handling what little money I had and my general day to day affairs (ex-wife, child support, CBS contracts, publishing agreements, tax arrangements). The manager asked the lawyer to explain my financial setup and what it was the lawyer was doing for me. Within fifteen minutes he'd punched a thousand holes in this guy's business acumen and generally shown the lawyer and me that he knew twice as much about law as did the lawyer. *I'm impressed.*

The next night the same thing with my accountant. By now I was not only impressed. I was *convinced*. From that point on, Stanley Polley took over my affairs. This was in April of 1969. By

December, I was already earning five times what I was the day I met him. He renegotiated my producer and artist contract with CBS. He renegotiated my publishing contract with Aaron Schroeder and got me back half my publishing. All my bills were paid out of the office; I didn't have to agonize over balancing a checkbook anymore. I felt great, and I was able to complete my album comfortably and confidently.

The new album was entitled, *You Never Know Who Your Friends Are*, a subtle shot at all the interesting press I had been receiving. The title song was a Beatlesque shuffle that included synthesizer programming by Walter Sear, one of the pioneers in the creation of the instrument. I wrote a song, "Magic In My Sox," that was inspired musically by a new group called CTA (soon to become "Chicago"; I'd heard 'em at the Whiskey in L.A. before they cut their first album) and lyrically by Henry Miller and *Portnoy's Complaint*. It's a narrative that has the singer holding a conversation with his penis. (Huh?) There's also a Harry Nilsson song called "Mourning Glory Story," which is a cappella with my friends Mike Gately, Robert John, Charlie Calello, myself, and Lou "Lightning Strikes" Christie singing a total of thirty-five voices through the miracles of modern recording.

Most of the album was cut with a band of between fifteen and twenty-six pieces (I don't know why I mention all this; the album's been out of print for years!). I wanted to duplicate this sound if I was to bother going out on the road to promote the album, and this was the first major problem I dumped into Stan Polley's lap. How to take a fifteen-piece band on the road and not lose your shirt.

Well, we had four things going for us. *Super Session, I Stand Alone, Child Is Father to the Man* (making a resurgence, thanks to BS&T's enormous popularity), and *Live Adventures* were all listed on *Billboard*'s Top Albums for about a month. This gave Stanley leverage to have me booked for good money, so it was feasible to actually take the band out.

A tour was confirmed for the summer of '69, and Calello and

I set about putting together Al's "dreamband." I wanted to get as many of the guys who played on the album as possible. We did some fast talking and got an incredible band together. It was Bernard "Pretty" Purdie on drums, Chuck Rainey on bass, Eric Gale on guitar, Dick Hyman on keyboards, Marvin Stamm, Ernie Royal, and Bernie Glow on trumpets, Billy Watrous, Jimmy Knepper, and Ray DeSio on trombones, George Young, Sol Schlinger, Joe Farrel, and Zoot Sims on saxes, Manny Green as leader and contractor, and Charles Calello, conductor and co-arranger. Many of these guys hadn't gone on the road in fifteen years, having chosen the relative ease and security of studio work. But they loved the arrangements that we wrote, they loved the music, and they loved the concept of a big band playing rock 'n' roll that was music. So they all went for it.

Our first gig was at a Teen Fair at the New York Coliseum. This was home ground, and everyone was real comfortable. It was also packed. The setup was that the band would warm up with a superfast jazz chart of "Hey Jude." There was room for all the soloists to strut their stuff and for everybody to air their chops out. Then they would start "Oh Happy Day," and halfway through I would come and finish the tune with them. After that, it was stuff from my two solo albums, *Super Session*, and BS&T, plus unrecorded stuff that I just dug playing. We used to close with a flagwaving version of "Proud Mary."

The show went down great, and afterward there was such a wall of kids outside the dressing room that we had to pull the old limousine escape trick. The Caddy was parked in the basement, and we ran offstage into an elevator and one minute later, I was two blocks gone toward home. I actually felt important for five whole minutes.

Nahh. It's all a crock of shit. So long as the people in the audience got their money's worth and enjoyed the music, that's what counts. I don't even like encores. I think you should get up there and play your little heart out for as long as you think they can stand it, and then split. It's a game. I'll usually only play an encore if I misjudge an audience. If I feel I'm losing them or that

I've overdone it, I try and split as fast as I can. There's never a planned middle to my shows. Only a beginning and an end. The middle is up to the audience. So if I think they've had enough and I'm *wrong*, I'll go back on. But encores by and large are self-indulgent.

The giant bigband was on the road throughout the summer of 1969. We played in Maryland, Oswego (huh?), Georgia, Massachusetts, Philadelphia, and finished up back in New York at Central Park.

The most exciting gig of the tour, and the best we ever played, was the Atlanta Pop Festival. It was July fourth and 110 degrees at this racetrack in the middle of nowhere. We arrived early afternoon and checked into the festival headquarters in downtown Atlanta. They provided us with a ballroom in which to rehearse, as we were carrying some alternate hornplayers this particular trip. (Sometimes Zoot Sims or Marvin Stamm couldn't make the gig, and Randy Brecker or Seldon Powell would sit in. Usually we didn't even have to rehearse. Charlie Calello would just talk them through it before the show, and they were pro enough to cut it.) So this time we ran down the show and then piled into a rent-a-bus and headed for the racetrack.

It was a together operation. The show was organized by old friend Chip Monck, the soon-to-be-famous "voice of Woodstock," who was undisputably the best stage setter around. He had music stands made up with cartoon Als on each one, and the lights were controlled on each music stand by a master dimmer built into the conductor's podium. Shit like that. It was *together*.

It was about 4:00 when we got there, and people were dropping like flies. The temperature, combined with bad acid going around, was keeping the medical tents SRO. Meanwhile, on stage a hell of a great show was going down. Janis Joplin, Canned Heat, Delaney & Bonnie, and Grand Funk were just some of the acts on the bill. Canned Heat was on when we arrived at the track, and we were scheduled next.

I hurriedly met with the promoters and asked if we could wait 'til the sun went down and cut the heat, as we had several senior citizens in the band and I was worried about their little hearts burning out in the blazing Georgia sun. They replaced us with Delaney & Bonnie, who played a blistering set featuring a then-searching Dave Mason on lead guitar. As they left the stage, I began to psyche up for the show. It took 'em forty minutes to set us up, and the sun had just set. The temperature dropped down at least ten degrees with the darkness, so it was only a hundred degrees now. *Jesus,* I thought, *let these guys live through this.* All the band were huddled in air-conditioned trailers backstage waiting until the last minute before they'd have to step into the sauna spotlight. Then it was time, and they hit the stage.

I paced around in the wings, anxious to get out there. I was standing with Bob Neuwirth, who was travelling with Janis Joplin, watching the audience respond to "Hey Jude." They weren't expecting anything like that, but they got off on it. Neuwirth kept lighting firecrackers and sparklers and flinging 'em around at everyone. I warned him about doing it around the hornplayers while we were on—I had enough trouble. He laughed.

Out I bounded onto the stage for my part of the show. There was an edge to the music I could sense right off. They were playing their asses off. The heat just made 'em get it on. I was exhausted trying to keep up with them. We played an extra fifteen minutes. I didn't want to give up the stage; I couldn't believe how great these guys were playing.

Finally, it was over and we left the stage. To say I was sweating, would be like saying Carol Doda has a tit or two. I couldn't breathe. I sat down on the steps of one of the trailers and all these people came around to congratulate me, but all they succeeded in doing was blocking me from breathing that good air. All of a sudden everything turned yellow and BONK! I just passed right out. The next thing I knew, Calello was unceremoniously pouring a bucket of icewater over my head. What a terrible way to come out of unconsciousness.

Meanwhile, the band was on the bus waiting for me. It seems

that we were booked on a flight that was scheduled to depart the Atlanta airport in two hours, and we had to leave right now to catch it. I sent the bus ahead, and me and Calello stayed behind so's I could get my airport legs. Some friendly freaks offered to drive us to the airport, and we took them up on their kindness. By the time we got there we'd struck up a friendship, so they walked us to the gate.

Right before we got there, all these redneck mechanics in their white jumpsuits were gathered together ogling the band. They took particular notice of me and the freaks. It looked like a potentially dangerous situation, circa 1966. I thought those days were over, but we *were* down South. I went to check in, and the guy at the gate told me I couldn't take that flight. Uh oh. Why, I inquired? Because you are not attired suitably to ride this plane. Snakeskin boots, satin pants, an Atlanta Pop Festival tee shirt, and a velvet jacket, all in various stages of drying off from Charlie's icewater bath. Admittedly, I looked a little disheveled, but I wasn't going to a fucking command performance for the queen. I was flying a stupid daily flight to Newark, and since when did you have to start dressing up to go to *Newark?* Meanwhile, the guys in the band were looking at me with a maybe-we-should catch-another-plane look in their eyes

Not *this* kid. Our contractor, Manny Green, was with us, and he happened to be a lawyer. He told the guy he wanted to see the supervisor post haste. Three minutes later, this Andy Griffith-character type ambles out. "Na whut seems to be the trubba, fallars?"

Manny explained how they won't let me on the plane, and how I'm the leader of this party of twenty-three. Tells him if I don't fly, then all twenty-three don't fly. Plus, we sue the airline for discrimination because after all they thought enough of me at one time to *sell* me twenty-three tickets . . . you get the idea.

Meanwhile, it was five minutes 'til blastoff. It ended up with the Andy Griffith clown making the gate attendant guy apologize to me and the band breaking into relieved applause and hurriedly boarding the plane. Me and Charlie, however, waited until it's one minute to takeoff, at which time I walked up to the gate guy in full view of the rednecks and tweaked his nose, emitted a loud *Yaarghh!* then raced down the walkway into the plane to a standing ovation. The doors closed a second later, and we made our way to lovely Newark without further incident. Just another day on the road, folks.

•

One day Clive Davis strolled into my office unannounced with one of my idols in tow: Don Ellis, the jazz trumpet whiz who, in my opinion, had taken up where Maynard Ferguson left off when he became an expatriate. Don was in town from his native California to select a producer for his next album, and he was interested in talking to me about it. I was extremely flattered.

Three days later we were in his band bus en route to the Tanglewood Festival in Massachusetts, so I could experience this band live. During the ride up, we discussed the goals Don was striving for with regard to his next album. We arrived five hours later and found that we were sharing the bill with the Modern Jazz Quartet and Judy Collins. They had Don scheduled to close the show, which surprised me considering the heavy company.

My surprise ended the moment his band walked out on stage. Don had a bitch of a group at that time, featuring John Klemmer on tenor, Frank Strozier on alto, Ray Neapolitan on bass, and Glenn Ferris on trombone. This was no ordinary band, even in attire. Don had the band outfitted by a hip L.A. boutique, and all twenty of them were resplendent in velvets and sequins. Then they played, and the audience, who could've pleaded weariness after sitting through two acts already, went nuts. Standing ovations and two encores. I swore that one of the things I *had* to do was record this band live. They were leaving for Europe the next day, but Don and I made plans to work on a new album when they returned.

Upon returning from Europe, the band was booked into Paul's Mall in Boston and then Stanford University in Palo Alto, California. We made arrangements ahead of time to record the

The National Safety Council advises, if you plan to ride your bicycle at night, wear something reflective. PHOTO: AL KOOPER COLLECTION.

Don Ellis surveying Kooper's damage to his music. Recording *Autumn,* Columbia Studios, Hollywood. PHOTO: FRED LOMBARDI, CBS.

band live at Stanford to get them hot off the European tour. Don was to arrive at Stanford a day early to work with me in setting things up.

When he arrived he was quite shaken. It seems the band had gotten to the Boston gig but their instruments had not. An airlines fuckup held the equipment overseas, forcing the band to sit in Boston while the gig had to be cancelled. Now they were desperately trying to reroute the lost instruments to Stanford in time for *this* concert and the live recording.

The remote truck from Wally Heider's studio was already on the way and could not be cancelled; the engineering crew was already checked in at the University Motel. The band *and* instruments arrived the next day, scant hours before the scheduled start of the concert, giving me a renewed five year subscription to my ulcers. The result of this hang-up was that the musicians were dying to play, itching to get ahold of the instruments that had been denied them for almost a week.

The concert was outdoors in an amphitheater at the school. We parked the truck behind the last row of the audience and ran our cable snakes the length of the place. While the concert was going on, I was racing back and forth, changing mike positions, listening in the truck, conferring with Don between songs, and doing all the other things that a producer does.

Recording a twenty-piece band outdoors is a producer's nightmare, and this was no exception. It was a helluva way to start my relationship with Don. With the aid of Columbia engineer Brian Ross-Myring, we were able to get an incredible audio diary of that concert, which, luckily, was one of the best Don played that year. We kept two tracks from the concert for the album: "Indian Lady" and "K.C. Blues." The remainder of the album was cut at Columbia Studios in Hollywood. It was released under the title *Autumn* in late 1969 and made top ten on the jazz charts. It was a privilege and a pleasure to work with someone as talented as Don Ellis.

•

Another of my productions that year was influenced by one of the favorite albums in my collection, *Cold Shot* by the Johnny

Otis Show on Kent Records. It featured the amazing guitar playing of Johnny's son Shuggie, only fourteen at the time. By some wonderful coincidence Epic Records (Columbia's sister label) had signed the Johnny Otis Show. I went down to talk with Larry Cohen, then president of Epic.

Larry was a true blues aficionado, had a huge record collection, and was the only legitimate blues-playing guitarist who was president of a major record company. I asked if it were possible to "borrow" Shuggie for one jam-type concept album. I wanted to do a follow-up to *Super Session* that would give a wider range of people a chance to hear this incredible underage virtuoso. Larry said it was OK with him, as long as it was OK with Poppa Johnny O.

That's all I had to hear. I was on the plane for L.A. the next day with the Otis residence address in my pocket. I met with Johnny and Shuggie, and they proved to be wonderful. Johnny was understandably protective of his son. After we all sat around and played for awhile, I knew he could see I meant no harm. I am told it was the first time he let Shuggie off on his own.

We flew back to New York and I put Shuggie up at my place. We listened to records all day for a week, choosing and weeding out the kinds of music we both enjoyed playing, and picked the borders of the album. I booked Stu Woods on bass and Wells Kelly on drums, two young white studio musicians who were knowledgeable in many different grooves. Mark "Moogy" Klingman sat in on keyboards on a few tracks, and in three or four days we had us an album.

BE: Stu Woods went on to fame recording and travelling with Janis Ian and Roberta Flack. Wells Kelly is currently a member of the rock group "Orleans." Klingman produced Bette Midler and was a member of Todd Rundgren's Utopia.

The goal was to get some incredible playing out of Shuggie, and we more than succeeded. You can listen to that album today, and time has not dulled the impact of this fifteen-year-old kid playing like a forty-five year old man!

The timing was remiss, however. Many people had jumped on the jam wagon, and the market was flooded with this kind of album. With no hit single on board, *Kooper Session Introducing Shuggie Otis* was a sales failure although a critical success. It remains one of my favorite albums.

•

As the year drew to a close, I could feel that a door was being shut. It wasn't until a few years later that I realized what an incredible musical entity the sixties had been and how slowed down the seventies seemed in comparison.

I mean, the Beatles, the sexual revolution, drugs, long hair, Kent State, the three assassinations, all in one decade. I thought that I had grown up in the fifties. But it was in the sixties that I really grew up. No matter how long I live, it will remain the most memorable ten years in my life (decadist that I am), and I hope you enjoyed sharing a little part of them with me.

Thanks for coming along.

PHOTO: ALICE OCHS

10

Loose Ends, Rolling Stones, Folk Singers, and the Boy Who Ate Dog Food

I guess this is the equivalent of an encore. However, it has many advantages over the rest of the set. It's a medley for one thing; you don't hafta sit through the whole song to hear the part you like. What's left over are a series of vignettes not necessarily in chronological order and completely disassociated with each other. They do, however, refer to and place themselves within certain time periods covered in the book previously.

Blacked Out in New York with the Mexicali Blues
November 9, 1965

One afternoon a friend and I dropped some organic mescaline and decided to go to the movies. We were in midtown Manhattan, and we chose the first-run *The Loved One*, a film I had already seen earlier in the week but was eager to see again, especially stoned.

We arrived at the theater about ten minutes after taking the mescaline, so we weren't high yet. About three-quarters through the show we're *really* loaded and all of a sudden the movie gets slower and slower and finally just stops altogether. I look at my friend and say, "I'm so high I can't even see the movie anymore."

He concurs and we realize that the movie has, in fact, prematurely stopped. An usher announces that the power will be restored in a moment. Just then another usher of Jamaican persuasion rushes in screaming, "Come see! De lights is out all over de damn city!"

Me and my friend laugh hysterically as everybody rushes to the street to check it out. They have to *coax* us out of our seats for a *few minutes* before we go. We are immediately transported into the middle of a powerless New York in the throes of rush hour at its peak. Heavy stuff.

My friend and I are quickly separated in a scene not unlike the climax of *Day of the Locust*. On my own, I get into a heavy Ray Bradbury trip, walk aimlessly for blocks and blocks, looking at all these weird situations. People stranded from commuting home crashed out by the hundreds in hotel lobbies. Coffee shops jammed with people eating by candlelight.

Then at the height of my high I get pushed into this bus. The bus is stopping at every block and people are forcing their way in the back doors and it's really panicsville. When the bus is as jammed as it can be, the driver passes up the lines at all the bus stops along his route. At every intersection he stops for the bus is violently attacked by frustrated standees who rock it back and forth in an attempt to get inside. By this time I'm in tears and people are looking at me like *I'm* crazy!

The bus, fortunately, is headed downtown and soon I'm in relatively familiar territory. I meet some folks I know, and we retire to their apartment. On the way we're watching junkies break into stores and cops trying to deal with them without using Gestapo tactics (New York cops are comparatively the sanest). Anyhow, my friends feed me, cool me out. I call home, cool my wife out, and tell her I'll return when the power does.

We then set out on a tour of Greenwich Village visiting friends, observing various psychodramas, and killing the whole night until we return to their apartment to crash. By this time I'm down from the mescaline and exhausted physically and mentally. I lay my head down on the pillow, shut my weary eyes,

BB King and Fido Bloomfield. PHOTO: AL KOOPER.

when the TV goes on, the radio goes on, the light over the bed goes on, the garbage disposal goes on, and frankly, it's the most horrendous sound ever heard as every appliance in New York swings back into action. I look at my nonelectric watch and note that it's almost twelve hours to the second since New York's famous black-out began. Far out, man.

The Boy Who Ate Dog Food

This one takes place in the period between the Blues Project and Blood, Sweat & Tears, when I was living in somebody's attic in Oakland, California. One day in an effort to relieve my boredom and anxiety, I went to Mill Valley to visit my friend Mike Bloomfield. We spent the day playing records and talking, and soon it was dark. Mark Naftalin, a buddy and playing mate of Mike's, dropped in, and the three of us sat in the kitchen trading stories about old blues players.

Michael's dog was lying on the kitchen floor crying the whole time we were sitting there. We were real stoned, having smoked the required fifty-seven joints that California people do in the course of a day (higher tolerance than New Yorkers). Maybe that's why I didn't notice right away that the "cookies" Michael was munching on while he talked about Howling Wolf, were *Fives,* a popular California brand of kibble for dogs and cats. I called this to his attention, secretly hoping his sense of *something* had been dulled temporarily by his stoned state.

"Oh no, man, I eat this all the time. 'S good. Want some?"

Sure.

When no one was looking, I snuck my handful down to the dog, and he stopped crying.

A Nice Place to Visit, But I Wouldn't Want to Die There

Around 1970, I was rounding out a nationwide tour with a few dates in the New York area. One concert was booked out at C. W. Post College in Greenvale, Long Island. It's the local equivalent of Miami U.—basket-weaving, etc. The last time I played at old C. W. was for their homecoming weekend of 1962–63. I was with a society orchestra on that date. Me and this other guy (his father was the bass player and the leader) would sit there with our guitars cradled in our arms while they somnambulated through "Laura," "A Foggy Day," etc. Then ten minutes out of every hour, we would jump up and play stuff they could twist to. Paul (the other guy) would sing lead, and I would play lead guitar backups. He got me the gig. It paid $50 a night which was good money for such little work. That was the only time I worked with Jerry Simon's orchestra, but I repeated the scenario with many local Welks. Jerry's son, Paul, later went on to become the shorter side of Simon and Garfunkel, but the boy do have *roots!*

Simon and Kooperfunkel, together again. PHOTO: GERALD JACOBSEN.

Anyway, here I was back at C. W., and at $5,000, I think they were paying me one hundred times what they paid me last time. Not bad for seven years' work. We're headlining this show with Long John Baldry and the J. Geils Band in support. I had seen the Geils band play a week earlier, and there was no way I was gonna follow them. I never dug headlining anyway. In a three-act show, it's hipper to go on second 'cause you get the audience in their prime. By the time the third act comes on they've sat through at least three hours of god-knows-what, and they're wasted. Also, if you headline, you gotta hang around all night long, and that is the lowest. It's strictly a matter of ego and management, but let me get in there, play and go home, I don't care if I open the damn show.

I strolled on down to Geils' dressing room while Baldry was onstage. Peter Wolf (lead singer) was an old friend of mine (used to interview me when he was a DJ in Cambridge, Massachusetts) and we said hi and all that shit. I asked them if they minded closing the show and they were glad to do it. It also let the show make more sense in terms of energy buildup. Baldry was into his last song, so I made it back to my dressing room to get ready. My folks had made one of their infrequent pilgrimages to hear their "darling son," and I wanted to get up there and "kick a little ass" for them.

Well, I was just slipping into my rhinestone-studded pants when the Man enters. Cops in the dressing room never bother me much, 'cause I'm not getting high at the time, and I don't have a police record (I didn't even know they made an album). Usually, they were nosing around for dope, so I'd ask them real complicated questions about their guns or boots until they'd get bored and leave. Well, tonight we had the chief of police of Greenvale, Long Island, and the head of security for C. W. Post College both in my dressing room at one time. I was honored.

"Mr. Kooper? Ah, yes. Well, it seems that someone has threatened to kill you tonight during your performance. They phoned headquarters to warn us, so I wouldn't put much credence into it, but nonetheless, what would you like to do about it?"

I told him I would like to get the fuck out of there as soon as possible. However, it was a sellout concert, I was the *advertised* headliner, and it's probably just some coked up guy whose old lady bought an Al Kooper album that day.

The chief informs me he's got thirty policemen (that was probably the whole fucking force) outside to assist if anything might occur. I told him to dismiss twenty-six of 'em; all we needed was four pall bearers. Heh, heh.

We're all yukking it up when I realize I gotta go onstage in five minutes. Target time. Not only that, but there's probably only *two* people *not* smoking dope in the audience (my folks), and a surprise appearance by thirty uniformed policemen would not endear me to the crowd, if you catch my drift. And the ole chief, he don't wanna start no riot for a few joints, bless his heart. Well, I says, let's put four plainclothesmen in front of the stage ready to rock, and let's do a quick escape motorcycle escort right after the last song, and fuck it, we'll roll the dice.

"Great, thank you, Mr. Kooper," and the cops is gone.

My sidemen at the time, John Paul Fetta on bass and Roy Markowitz (husband to Laurel Masse of Manhattan Transfer) on drums, were more scared than I was. And I was gettin' real scared. As we walked out, no *ran* out on stage, I realized that my parents were out there somewhere, and that gave it a kind of John Frankenheimer reality. (*New York Post* the next day, "And as his horrified parents Samuel and Natalie watched in helpless horror, a volley of bullets caught him in the chest right in the middle of 'Season of the Witch,' toppling him to the stage floor. At first the crowd thought it was part of the show, but when thirty police officers began to . . .")

Well, we didn't play too well. I kept staring around everywhere looking for glints, tramps, and grassy knolls, and my mind was not on the music. We went over surprisingly well, did an encore (they deserved it after such a mediocre show), and then tore-ass off stage. Three cops immediately grabbed me and "escorted me to an already moving vehicle" (shades of Dylan) with a motorcycle escort to the Long Island Expressway.

P.S. I didn't get killed. I didn't even get shot at, not a stab wound or any wet noodle marks. I did, however, cut my performance schedule down from fifty appearances a year to fifteen and decided to stick to small clubs. But don't get me wrong, I love my country. You meet the nicest people there.

Blond on Blonde or A Jew's Dues in Nashville

When I was in the Blues Project, I was given a sabbatical in early '66 to rejoin Dylan in the studio and assist in the recording of a new album. Bob Johnston, a Southerner, who was his producer at the time, suggested that Bob try cutting some of the album in Nashville with some of the best musicians the town had to offer. Bob agreed, but stipulated that Robbie Robertson and myself join whatever cast was assembled. I had never been down south before and was not particularly looking forward to it due to various accounts I had perused in the papers. However, Johnston met us at the airport and had secured the service of one

"And this item was actually one of Donovan's diapers." With Dylan and Doug Sahm. PHOTO: ALICE OCHS.

of Elvis's bodyguards for the duration of the visit just in case Nashville folk weren't "ready" for Dylan. Mr. Lamar Fike was introduced to us, and he spent the two weeks that we were there telling us what life was like with Elvis. Actually, Lamar was a great guy with a *nasty* sense of humor.

One day, with some time off, I ventured out of our protective web on a shopping expedition to Buckley's, the largest record store in town. I decided to make it on foot from the hotel, as it was a nice day and it was just a straight walk down the main drag about three-quarters of a mile from the hotel.

About halfway there, there's a bunch of kids hanging out on the corner looking for trouble or me, whichever came first, I thought to myself. They were about eighteen–nineteen years old, but real mean looking; about three of 'em. I didn't even have what you would call long hair then; I actually looked straight. Had on black Beatle boots, black pants, shirt and tie for good measure, and a black leather car coat. This was my basic uniform in that era.

I decide to cross the street so as not to even walk past their line of vision. I'm runnin' across the street to make the light and right off they're imitating my run as they spin off after me. I should've continued running, but I didn't know if it *was* early enough to commit myself to my paranoia. It was. All of a sudden, there's a hand on my shoulder.

Now, it's mid-day in downtown Nashville, there's lots of people and traffic in the street and it's the main drag, but inherently, I know that if these guys start wasting me, nobody's gonna pay much attention, 'specially if they hear me say "Ow" with a Yankee accent. Also, in case you haven't met me, let me explain that I was never a contender in the Golden Gloves. I'm about six-foot-one and weight about 145. In short, a meek, walking toothpick.

So this hand is on my shoulder spinning me around, and the reality is hitting me: if I don't nail the first guy first, I'll be going straight to Nashville General. Just as he's about to say something funny at the conclusion of the spin-around, I slam my fist into his groin. He hit the dirt groaning.

His friends, deciding that valor was the better part of punkdom, stood their ground, and it was sort of status quo for a second as we all turned into chickens. I started tear-assing down the boulevard looking for sanctuary and a telephone. About two or three blocks down, I found a well-populated bookstore and barreled into the phone booth. I called Al Grossman's (Dylan's manager) room and told him what was happening and where I was. He said sit tight, they'd be there in a minute.

I hoped so, because here come the punks to the outside of the store. They spot me in the phone booth and set up guard outside the door, figuring I gotta go some time. Trusting in Grossman, I edge out of the phone booth and pretend to browse around the bookstore. *Mistake.* In comes one heading right for me. I can see it all now; books flying, jail cells, death notices. Just as the guy enters the shop, here comes Lamar in a fat Caddy screeching to a halt in front of the shop. He jumps out of the car, spots me through the window, then casually strolls into the store. The kid heads right for me, and my adrenaline is at the bursting point. I grab him by his collar and say, "Look, you motherfucka, you and your friends get the fuck off my back or I'm gonna get MAD!"

He looks at me incredulously just as Lamar rounds the corner and pulls me off the punk saying, "Al, you better stop picking fights, I'm tired of bailing your ass outa jail every other day," and all the while we're edgin' outa the shop. The kid is still thinkin' what the fuck? as we dive into the Caddy and head back to the hotel, hysterical.

•

The combination of Dylan, his current material, and the Nashville musicians was near-perfect. There was me and Robbie, Charlie McCoy, and Henry Strzelecki on bass, Wayne Moss, Charlie McCoy, Jerry Kennedy, Joe South on guitars, Hargus "Pig" Robbins on keyboards, and Kenny Buttrey on drums. They were extremely flattered to have Dylan in their midst and gave him every consideration they could. The janitor emptying ashtrays at the sessions turned out, in later years, to be a young struggling Kris Kristofferson.

We worked at Columbia Studios. Dylan had sketches of most of the songs, but he completed the bulk of the writing there in Nashville, most of it in the studio. When he felt like writing or rewriting, everyone would repair to the ping-pong tables in the canteen. Sometimes, in the case of "Sad Eyed Lady of the Lowlands" or "Visions of Johanna," he would sit in there for five hours without coming out and just play the piano and scribble. He had a piano put in his hotelroom, and during the day I would sit and play the chords to a song he was working on while he tried different sets of lyrics to them. It was good 'cause I got the jump on the tunes and was able to teach them to the band that night without Dylan being bothered with that task. There were some little things about the sessions that were funny.

There was this keyboard player named Pig. He looked like your everyday plumber or executive (late thirties, scrubbed Wasp look) except he was blind. He was so unuptight about the situation that after awhile you would forget it.

Dylan had this problem with him. He couldn't talk directly to him because he couldn't call this sweet guy Pig. So he would say to someone else (usually yours truly) " . . . and tell the piano player to play an octave higher." And he would look in Pig's direction and sorta smile, 'cause that way he avoided calling him Pig.

The definitive Pig story is told by Bob Johnston. Seems that Pig and the boys tied one on one night after a late session, and they're driving home when this uncontrollable urge comes over the inebriated Pig.

"I wanna drive. You so-and-so's move over and let me navigate this Cadillac!"

His buddies, bein' drunker than Pig, pulled the car over and put Pig in the driver's seat. In a moment they were goin' down the highway with a blind driver and a car fulla drunk rednecks. The guy ridin' shotgun is sayin', "A little to the left . . . good . . . uh, now a little to the right . . . a little faster . . . " and they're actually pulling it off until they see a red light flashin' behind 'em and the familiar siren of the Tennessee Highway Patrol. They get

Pig to pull the car over, and that's where the story ends. The rest is left up to the listener's imagination, if he can think. Usually, he's laughing too hard.

•

One time I fell asleep on the soft carpet floor of the studio while Dylan was deep into writing. I was awakened by Dylan shaking me. All the musicians were sitting around me, instruments poised, waiting to record. "C'mon, Al, you're holding up the whole session. Everyone's waiting for you!! Hey, wake up!" Real embarrassing.

Another night I was sitting in the control booth while Dylan was in the studio unmoving, writing again. Al Grossman had made a habit of pitching quarters into the soundproofed ceiling, and now everyone was doing it. I just knew when we left town, some engineer was gonna turn up a bass track all the way and all them fuckin' quarters was gonna rain down on the control room like a Las Vegas jackpot.

Anyway, me and Grossman and Johnston are pitchin' quarters, and this local newspaperman had somehow got in. He was in there about an hour and a half just staring at the motionless Dylan through the glass when he finally said, "Damn! What's he on, anyhow?"

Grossman, not wanting the facts to get distorted in this guy's potential scoop, tells him "Columbia Records, sir." The guy is ushered out shortly thereafter.

•

Dylan was teachin' us a song one night when Johnston suggested it would sound great Salvation Army style. Dylan thought it over and said it might work. But where would we get hornplayers at this hour? "Not to worry," says Charlie McCoy and grabs the phone. It's 4:30 A.M. when he makes the call. Now I am not exaggerating when I say that at 5:00 A.M. in walks a trombone player. He's clean-shaven, wearing a dark suit and tie, wide awake and eager to please ... and ... he's a helluva trombone player. He sat down and learned the song, they cut three takes, and at 5:30 he was out the door and gone.

Charlie McCoy blew my mind many times that trip, but my fondest memory was when we were recording "You Go Your Way I'll Go Mine." There was a little figure after each chorus that he wanted to put in on trumpet, but Dylan is not fond of overdubbing. It was a nice lick, too. Simple, but nice. Now Charlie was already playing bass on the tune. So we started recording and when that section came up, he picked up a trumpet in his right hand and played the part while he kept the bass going with his left hand without missing a lick in either hand. Dylan stopped in the middle of the take and just stared at him in awe. It's on the record with no overdubbing two takes later; bass and trumpet! This guy is everything great you ever heard about him. If it makes music, he can play it.

The credits are vague on the *Blond on Blonde* album. Maybe I can fill in a few holes for the reader. Joe South is playing bass on "Visions of Johanna." He has a very special style of playing bass, sort of hillbilly funk. His unique guitar style is most discernible in the mix on "Memphis Blues Again." He and I have some nice organ-guitar trade-offs in that one. Wayne Moss plays the cool guitar parts on "I Want You."

The other amazing thing about cutting that album was the firsthand knowledge that you were making history. After I cut the *Highway 61* album, I heard those songs everywhere. I will probably hear them all my life, anywhere I go. They are instant classics because they are prime Dylan. Imagine how it felt playing on a session when, by virtue of the fact that you had already done it once, you knew that whatever you played would last *forever*. That's a heavy feeling and a heavy responsibility for a punk from Queens, New York. Thank you, Bob, for giving me that opportunity.

Like a Rolling Stone in London

Around the time I finished the *Live Adventures* album, I was feeling real overworked and was sick of being in a studio day after day. I called close friend, Denny Cordell, producer of Joe Cocker, Procul Harum, and the legendary Move, who lived in London. "I wanna come over for awhile to rest from the studio. Pick us up at the airport and don't tell a soul that we're coming. It's escape time!"

Denny is an incredible character and deserves a chapter all his own, but that's another book in another place. So he meets me and my wife, Joanie, at the airport. How was the flight, blah, blah. He said that the Stones' office had called him and did I feel like playing a few sessions with them? Oh, no. Not the studio again. I mean it's really an honor and all that, but why did Raquel Welch wait until I fucked every chick in town before she snuck up to my room, if you catch my drift.

We got dropped at our hotel and just crashed out from the flight the first day. How did they know I was coming to town? I wondered. So the next day we're shopping on Kings Road, and we bump into Brian Jones in a shirt store. "Are you gonna play the session, Al?" *How can you say no to these people?*

They wanted me for two sessions. I decided to do one and if it was really fun, rock on; if it wasn't groovy, I'd get an ulcer attack the next night. I think the reason they called me was that their regular keyboard player was in the States at the time (Nicky Hopkins). As usual I got to the studio early. Charlie and Bill arrived next. I had met them before with Dylan. First-rate no-nonsense nice guys. It was good to see them again. I was sitting at the organ sort of nervously doodling around 'til everyone was there but Mick and Keith. Jimmy Miller, an American, was the producer. We exchanged amenities.

Just then Mick and Keith came exploding in the door. Mick is wearing a gorilla coat, and Keith's got on this sort of Tyrolean hat with a real long feather in it. It was gonna be party time, and they were the party from the moment they arrived. Everyone sat around on the floor with either an acoustic guitar or a percussion instrument, and Mick and Keith played the song they wanted to record until everyone had the chord changes and the rhythm accents. There was a conga player there who could play congas and roll huge hash joints without missing a lick. It was decided I would play piano on the basic track and overdub organ later.

I got into this groove I had heard on an Etta James record of "I Got You Babe" that really fit their song well. Keith picked up on it right away and played a nice guitar part that meshed right with it. While they were getting the sounds they wanted on the instruments, Jimmy Miller was telling Charlie a certain accent he thought would do the song up. Charlie just couldn't seem to get the part and stepped down unhappily to take a break. Jimmy Miller sat down at the drums and remained there playing drums on the take! Charlie was real dejected. Mick and Keith played acoustic guitars, I played piano, Bill on bass, and Brian Jones lay on his belly in the corner reading an article on botany through the whole proceedings.

When a proper take was gotten, Keith overdubbed an electric part and I overdubbed the organ. After about four hours of recording, two men showed up with long folding tables and set up a veritable beggars' banquet with rack of lamb, curries, vegetables, rices, salads, a large selection of wines, and lots of different desserts. Quite a change from a cheeseburger break in the States. I was so full after all that, I almost fucked up the organ part. I had a great time playing, and I was treated real nicely, so I was actually looking forward to the next evening's session.

The song we recorded the first night was "You Can't Always Get What You Want," which later appeared on the *Let It Bleed* album and was also the flipside of the single, "Honky Tonk Woman." Almost nine months after that session, an eight-track master of the song arrived at my office one day at CBS. There was a note which said: *"Dear Al, you once mentioned you could put some great horn parts on this. Well, go ahead and do it and send us the tape back. Love, Mick."*

What a memory that Jagger has. I wrote out a horn chart, leaving a spot in the intro where I could play a French horn solo. The intro itself took me three hours to get 'cause I'm not the world's greatest French horn player, and I wanted to sound like I was. I could never have done it at all without the coaching of one of the best hornplayers in the country, Ray Alonge—thank you, Ray. Then I put the rest of the horns on with studio cats. It was a bad night in the studio for me, and the part didn't come out nearly as good as I thought it might. I crossed my fingers and sent Mick back his tape. A year later it came out, and they had ditched all the horn parts except my little French horn intro. It sounded fantastic on the radio, you could hear the piano and the organ, and they actually gave me credit on the single. Nice guys in spite of their image. (Wot image, mate?)

The next night we cut a track from the film Jagger was currently working on, *Performance*. The song was called "Memo from Turner," but was not the version used in the film or on the soundtrack album. I believe it was issued on a later London album of outtakes. I played one other time with them a few years later at a birthday party for Keith at Olympic Studios in London. They were working on the *Sticky Fingers* album. After the party, they cleared away the debris and set up to record. They cajoled Eric Clapton, myself, and Bobby Keys to join them in a previously unheard tune called "Brown Sugar." George Harrison, who was among the party goers, was invited to play but declined. I read somewhere in an interview with Keith that it came out great and that they would release it someday, but the version on *Sticky Fingers* is another one entirely. I must take this opportunity to say that over the years, the Stones have always been honorable, great people to hang out with, and the best people to play after-hours music with.

How She Got Herself to the Garden in the First Place

One night in the middle of the Blues Project, I was sitting in my favorite bar in the Village, the Dugout. It was the best place to kill a summer's night, and I always ran into a few friends I would miss while I was on the road. This particular night I was sitting with a new-girl-in-town, who we shall call Joanie.

Joanie had a crush on Roy Blumenfeld, the drummer from the Blues Project. Unfortunately for her, Roy had a girlfriend who was hip to Joanie and real jealous of her. So, this chick is crying in my beer for about three hours, and I don't mind 'cause she's real cute and nothing else is going on anyway. So they're closing the bar and throwing us out and I offer to walk her home. It was about a fifteen minute stroll, and it was a beautiful summer's night. I was, in fact, homeless at the time, crashing out at Judy Collins' apartment, and glad to have my mind taken off that situation.

When we got to her door, she invited me in to hear some of her new songs. She was a folksinger. Canadian. Half of a duet with her recently divorced husband, and they had achieved a mild popularity and a cult following in various American border cities. She, being sorta pretty, had me bounding up the stairs figuring if the songs were lousy, maybe I could salvage the evening some other way. In a few minutes that became the furthest thing from my mind.

Her songs were incredible and totally original, which was a surprise in those days, but quite refreshing. She would finish one, and I would say more, more. And she had enough to keep going for four hours, most of them brilliant. One song especially killed me, and I thought it would be great for Judy Collins, and a nice way to pay her for her hospitality would be to turn her on to it. Being impulsive, I asked Joanie if I could use her phone and I called Judy up. It was 5:30 A.M. by now, and she was sort of pissed off.

"I have to get up soon and drive all the way to the Newport

Folk Festival, and I wanted to get some sleep for a change. I could hear this song when I get back from the festival though, Al."

Bong! A great idea hits me. "Judy, why don't you, room permitting, take this girl with you to the festival. She could play the song and others for you on the way up and make your trip that much more pleasant. Then, being that you're on the board of directors, you could see if maybe they could fit her in the schedule somewhere to play, huh?"

Silence.

"Judy?"

"Kooper, you bastard. Yeah, I'll do it. Gimmee her number. Bye."

Just to make sure, I gave Joanie Judy's number and told her to call her in a couple of hours. I split immediately 'cause I was exhausted and never made it to Judy's place, preferring to actually crash on a bench in Washington Square Park in the steamy, summer morning.

Well, as the saying goes, the rest is history. Joanie (Joni Mitchell, of course) played at the festival (1967) and stole the whole show. Judy eventually recorded the song I thought she would like, "Michael From the Mountains," and also had a huge hit with "Both Sides Now," another of Joni's songs. Joni never thanked me, but when I heard the album *Ladies of the Canyon* that was thanks enough. Maybe I should thank her.

Sweet Judy Blue Eyes

This ain't no funny story or starstruck kid here, just an appreciation of a friend: Judy Collins.

As I mentioned, I lived at her apartment off and on in 1967. She was *always* helping somebody out, and she was the real New York Earth Mother. If you were an up-and-coming writer, she would always be one of the first to showcase your material. If you had a fight with your lover, she would be the trusted confidante of both sides. Her apartment was the social hub of folk music on the East Coast. Eric Andersen, David Blue, Phil Ochs, Joan Baez, Mimi Farina, Tom Paxton, Joni Mitchell, Bob Dylan, Donovan, Pete Seeger, Steve Stills (who wrote "Judy Blue Eyes Suite" for her) would all have nothing but superlatives to say about the lady.

I haven't seen her in awhile. Time and space have kept us apart physically, but I feel together with her spiritually. As Bernie Taupin says: "It's for people like you that I keep it turned on." * *Thank you for everything.*

A Farewell to Palms or The Amazing Jewish Rubber Plant

Every day at 6:15 P.M. when I worked at CBS, some guy would come around and water the plant in my office. I know I mentioned this before, but this is different. This was his gig and he was so bored with it that he never even looked at the damn things. He just poured in his two ounces and split. When I found I no longer worked there anymore, I replaced the plant with a plastic one that looked just like it. And sure enough, every day, and probably to this very day, the guy comes in and waters this fake plant. What a wonderful way to end the book.

---

* Copyright © 1969 Dick James Music Limited. Used by permission. All rights reserved.

Hope you enjoyed the ride. PHOTO: SAM KOOPER.

Discography

1. "Sick Manny's Gym." Leo De Lyon & The Musclemen. Musicor 45.
2. "This Diamond Ring." Gary Lewis & The Playboys. Liberty.
3. "I Must Be Seeing Things." Gene Pitney. Musicor.
4. *Highway 61 Revisited.* Bob Dylan (played organ & piano). Columbia.
5. *Take a Little Walk with Me.* Tom Rush (Electric guitar & piano). Elektra.
6. *Album.* Peter, Paul and Mary. (Organ on "Well, Well, Well"). Warner Brothers.
7. *What's Shakin'.* Various Artists. ("I Can't Keep from Cryin' Sometimes" vocals, piano & electric guitar). Elektra.
8. *The Blues Project Live at the Cafe Au GoGo.* Verve/Folkways.
9. *Blond on Blonde.* Bob Dylan. (Piano and organ). Columbia.
10. *Projections.* The Blues Project. Verve/Folkways.
11. *Electric Ladyland.* Jimi Hendrix. (Piano on "Long Hot Summer Nights."). Warner Brothers.
12. *The Who Sell Out.* (Organ on "Rael"). Decca.
13. *The Blues Project Live at Town Hall.* Verve/Forecast.
14. *Ellis Island.* Paupers. (Piano and organ). MGM.
15. *Changes.* Jim & Jean. (Lead guitar on "Stranger in a Strange Land" and electric harpsichord on "Changes"). Verve/Forecast.
16. *Child Is Father to the Man.* Blood, Sweat & Tears. Columbia.
17. *Wow/Grape Jam.* Moby Grape. (Piano). Columbia.
18. *Super Session.* Bloomfield-Kooper-Stills. Columbia.
19. *I Stand Alone.* Al Kooper. Columbia.

246 | Discography

20. *The Live Adventures of Mike Bloomfield & Al Kooper.* Columbia.
21. "You Can't Always Get What You Want"/"Memo From Turner." Rolling Stones. London Records.
22. *You Never Know Who Your Friends Are:* Al Kooper. Columbia.
23. *Kooper Session Introducing Shuggie Otis.* Columbia.
24. *Autumn.* Don Ellis. (Production). Columbia.
25. *Appaloosa.* (Production). Columbia.
26. *Sweet Linda Divine.* (Production). Columbia.
27. *Easy Does It.* Al Kooper. Columbia.
28. *New York City (You're a Woman).* Al Kooper. Columbia.
29. *The Sweetheart Sampler.* Frankie & Johnny. (Production). Warner Brothers.
30. *Gately's Cafe.* Michael Gately. (Production). Janus Records.
31. *A Possible Project of the Future/Childhood's End.* Al Kooper. Columbia.

(Productions)

32. Lynyrd Skynyrd. (Pronounced Leh-nerd Skinn-nerd.) "Sounds of the South."
33. *Get Right.* Mose Jones. "Sounds of the South."
34. *Reunion in Central Park.* The Blues Project. "Sounds of the South."
35. *Naked Songs.* Al Kooper. Columbia.
36. *Second Helping.* Lynyrd Skynyrd. "Sounds of the South."
37. *Sweet Home Alabama.* Lynyrd Skynyrd. MCA.
38. *Mose Knows.* Mose Jones. MCA.
39. *Nuthin' Fancy.* Lynyrd Skynyrd. MCA.
40. *The Tubes.* A&M.
41. *Cry Tough.* Nils Lofgren. A&M.
42. *Act Like Nothing's Wrong.* Al Kooper. United Artists.

Index

A & M Records, 18
Abramson, Marc, 78
Adelphi Studios, 18, 37
Adler, Lou, 139, 141
Aldon Music, 17-18, 45, 46
Allman, Gregg, 114
Anastasia, Phil, 29-30
Anderle, David, 139, 141, 142, 144, 148-49
Anderson, Eric, 62, 84, 155, 156, 243
Animals, 111
Anonymous Artists of America, 196
Antioch College, 97, 98-99
Arc publishing empire, 16
Aristocats, 31
Arnold, Jerome, 60, 90
Atlanta Pop Festival, 215-16
Atlantic Records, 18, 158, 188
Auger, Brian, 188
Autumn, 221

Bacharach, Burt, 34
Baez, Joan, 149, 150, 243
Baldry, Long John, 230
"Ballad of a Thin Man," 66
Band, The, 162, 204
Barksdale, Everett, 76
Barry White Publishing Catalogue, 18
Basie, Count, 77
Beach Boys, 139, 146
Beatles, 17, 46, 108, 116
Beck, Jeff, 193

Berg, John, 208
Bernstein, Sid, 118, 133, 182
Berry, Chuck, 16, 77, 96, 102, 108, 120, 124
Big Brother and the Holding Company, 144, 162, 168
Big Sur Folk Festival, 149, 150
Bishop, Elvin, 88, 174, 200-202, 206
Bitter End, 124, 173
Blond on Blonde, 99, 206, 237
Blood, Sweat & Tears, 160-79, 185, 191, 206, 208, 212
Bloomfield, Mike, 54, 60, 61, 79, 88, 129, 130, 148, 185-86, 190, 194, 196, 197-98, 227-28
Bloomfield, Susie, 148, 198
Blue, David, 62, 79, 108, 243
"Blues Bag, The," 92-94
Blues Image, 168
"Blues Part IV," 206
Blues Project, The, 80-134, 141, 185, 232
Blues Project, The, 83
Blues Project Live at the Cafe Au GoGo, The, 100
Blues Project Live at Town Hall, The, 108
Blues Singers, The, 204
Blumenfeld, Roy, 79, 83, 87, 96, 108, 241
Booker T., 204
Brass, Bob, 38-42, 46
Brecker, Randy, 159, 176, 215

| **247**

248 | Index

Bridgeport, University of, 35-37
Brill Building, 15-17
Bringing It All Back Home, 50
Broadway, 15-19
Brooks, Harvey, 61, 66, 78, 148, 185, 188, 190
Brown, James, 19, 164
Browne, Jackson, 150
Bruce, Jack, 79, 125
Bruce, Lenny, 18, 90
Buckley, Tim, 165
Buffalo Springfield, 137, 144, 148, 188
Burrell, Kenny, 112
Butterfield, Paul, 60, 61, 88
Butterfield Blues Band, 79, 88-90, 129, 130, 185
Buttrey, Kenny, 206, 234
Byrds, 111, 137, 144, 168

Cafe Au GoGo, 90-94, 100, 124, 130, 155, 159, 160, 173
Cafe Interlude, 51-53
Calello, Charlie, 193-94, 211, 213-14, 215, 216
California, 137-53
California, Randy, 188
Canned Heat, 144, 168, 215
Casey, Al, 52-53
Cassidy, Ed, 153
Casuals, 22
"Catch the Wind," 88, 96
Cato, Bob, 168, 202, 208
CBS. *See* Columbia Records
Chambers Brothers, 150, 183
Charles, Ray, 19
Charmatz, Bill, 208
Chase, Jeff, 84, 96, 117
Cheap Thrills, 162
Chester, Gary, 76
Chicago, 213
Chicago Loop, 125
Chiffons, 19
Child Is Father to the Man, 168, 213
Chiriowski, Josef, 129
Christie, Lou, 213

Clapton, Eric, 79, 126, 240
Clark, Dick, 30
Clayton-Thomas, David, 179
Coasters, 78
Cobb, Willie, 190
Cocker, Joe, 238
Cohen, Larry, 222
Cold Shot, 221-22
Collectors, 193
Collins, Judy, 78, 79, 83, 142, 150, 153, 155, 156, 218, 241-44
Colomby, Bobby, 156, 157, 159, 163-64, 166, 167, 169, 172, 175, 176, 179
"Colored Rain," 206
Coltrane, John, 116
Columbia Records, 79, 84, 90, 102, 158, 159, 181-209, 213
Cooder, Ry, 153
Coolidge, Rita, 142
Cooper, Alice, 130
Cordell, Denny, 238
Cotton, James, 120, 168
Court, John, 77
Cream, 125, 126, 168
Crosby, David, 70, 148
Crystals, 34
CTA, 213
C. W. Post College, 228, 230-31

Daltrey, Roger, 126
Daniels, Charlie, 206
Darin, Bobby, 16
Davis, Clive, 158-59, 181, 184, 218
Davis, Jessie Ed, 153
Davis, Spencer, 182
Dean, Walter, 181, 184
"Dear Mr. Fantasy," 175, 204
Delaney & Bonnie, 215, 216
DeLyon, Leo, 31
Derby Steak House, 140
DeSio, Ray, 214
Diamond, Neil, 18
Diddely, Bo, 78
Dion & the Belmonts, 30
Dixon, Willy, 16

Index | 249

Doheny, Ned, 150
Donovan, 88, 96, 188, 243
"Don't Take Candy from a Stranger," 115
Doors, 78
Doubleday, Marcus, 148
Drifters, 45
Driscoll, Julie, 188
Dronge, Mark, 116
Dugout, 124
Dylan, Bob, 17, 46, 47, 49-51, 53-56, 59-70, 72, 165, 183, 185, 232, 234-37, 243

Electric Flag, 149, 173, 185, 190
Elektra Records, 78, 79, 83, 142, 149, 182
Eli and the 13th Confession, 193
Elliot, Ramblin' Jack, 62
Ellis, Don, 206, 218-21
Entwhistle, John, 126
Epic Records, 222
Ertegun, Ahmet, 18, 188
Ervin, Dee, 18
Even Dozen Jug Band, The, 83

Fabian, 29
"Fakin' It," 162
Family Dogg, 124, 168
Farina, Mimi, 118, 150, 166, 243
Farina, Richard, 118
Farrel, Joe, 214
"Feelin' Groovy," 204
Ferguson, Maynard, 147, 218
Ferris, Glenn, 218
Fetta, John Paul, 231
Fielder, Jim, 148, 149, 155, 156, 159
Fields, Danny, 182
Fike, Lamar, 233, 234
Filmore, 124, 194, 197-200
"Fire and Water," 129
Five Stairsteps, 28
Flack, Roberta, 222

Flanders, Tommy, 84, 87, 90, 94-96, 100
"Flute Thing, The," 112-14
"Fly Away," 102, 112
Follow-up songs, 39
Forest Hills concert, 64-66
Four Seasons, 193
Franklin, Aretha, 18, 183
Freed, Alan, 18
Freed, Lance, 18

Gale, Eric, 76, 214
Gallagher, Bill, 158
Gallico, Al, 99
Garcia, Jerry, 188, 200
Garfunkel, Artie, 144, 149, 150
Garrett, Snuff, 45
Garrick Theater, 173, 179
Gaslite, 62, 144
Gately, Mike, 213
Geils, J., 230
Generation Club, 159, 160, 173
Gescheidt, Alfred, 168
Getz, Stan, 90, 96
Getz Au Gogo, 90
Gibson, Henry, 53
Glan, Penti, 129
Gleason, Ralph J., 150
Glow, Bernie, 214
"God Only Knows," 146
Goffin, Jerry, 18, 165
"Goin' Down Louisiana," 110, 133
Gold, Wally, 182-83
Gold albums, 191
Goldberg, Barry, 60, 129, 148, 186
Goldner, George, 18
"Good Vibrations," 146
Goodman family, 16
Graham, Bill, 124, 168, 194, 197, 198-200
Grand Funk, 215
Grape, Moby, 160, 183
Grape Jam, 190
Grateful Dead, 22, 144, 196
Gravenites, Nick, 148

250 | Index

Great Society, 124
Green, Debby, 62
Green, Manny, 214, 217
"Green Onions," 204
Greenfield, Howie, 18
Gregg, Bobby, 61, 78
Gribble, Jim, 27-30
Griffin, Paul, 56
Grossman, Albert, 59, 64, 66, 88, 234, 236
Grossman, Stefan, 83
Guercio, James William, 179
Guy, Buddy, 190

Halligan, Dick, 159, 179
Hammond, John, Jr., 144, 183
Hammond, John, Sr., 183
Hancock, Herbie, 183
Handy, John, 169
Hardly Worthit Players, 125
Harris, Paul, 120
Harrison, George, 19, 240
Harum, Procul, 238
"Harvey's Tune," 190
Havens, Richie, 108
Hawkins, Ronnie, 61
Hawks, 61, 72
Heider, Wally, 196, 221
Helm, Levon, 61, 72
Henderson, Jill, 112
Henderson, Sally, 153
Hendrix, Jimi, 144, 160, 193
Hentoff, Nat, 80
"Heroes and Villains," 146
"He's So Fine," 19
"Hey, Jude," 214, 216
Highway 61 Revisited, 61, 75, 185, 188, 237
Hoh, Eddie, 185, 188
Holiday, Billie, 183
Hollywood Bowl concert, 69-70
Holzman, Jac, 78, 142
Hood, Clarence, 62
Hook, Jack, 18
Hooker, John Lee, 92, 93, 108

Hopkins, Nicky, 238
House, Son, 87
"House in the Country," 166-68
Howling Wolf, 16, 120
Hutton, Danny, 139
Hyman, Dick, 115, 214

"I Ain't Marchin' Anymore," 79
Ian, Janis, 222
"I Can't Keep from Crying," 79, 116
"I Can't Quit Her," 149, 158, 162
Iggy & The Stooges, 168
"I'll Keep It with Mine," 79
"I Love You More Than You'll Ever Know," 164, 168
Imhoff, Barry, 159
"I Must Be Seeing Things," 46
"Indian Lady," 221
"I Need to Fly," 158
In Sound—From Way Out, The, 114
Iron Butterfly, 148
Isley Brothers, 18
"I Stand Alone," 208-9, 213
"It's All Over Now Baby Blue," 60
"It Takes a Lot to Laugh, It Takes a Train to Cry," 190
"I Wanna Be Your Driver," 96

Jabberwock, 153
Jackie The K Dancers, 125
Jagger, Mick, 238-40
James, Billy, 102, 182
James, Etta, 239
James Gang, 129
Jan & Dean, 21
Jarmells, 38
Jefferson Airplane, 144
Jeremy & The Satyrs, 168
Jim and Jean, 79, 125
John, Robert, 213
Johnson, Blind Willie, 79, 87
Johnston, Bob, 206, 232, 235, 236
Johnston, Don, 172
Jones, Brian, 142, 143, 238, 239

Joplin, Janis, 144, 168, 215, 216
"Just One Smile," 34, 165

Kahn, John, 194, 198
Kalb, Danny, 83, 84, 87, 94, 96, 104, 106, 107, 108, 111, 116, 130, 133
Katz, Steve, 83, 87, 94, 96, 100, 106, 107, 112, 125, 140, 156, 157, 159, 164, 165-66, 167, 170, 172, 176
"K.C. Blues," 221
Kelly, Wells, 222
Kennedy, Jerry, 206, 234
Kettle of Fish, 62
Keys, Bobby, 240
King, BB, 87, 93, 120, 160, 173-74
King, Ben E., 165
King, Carole, 18, 165
King Curtis, 75
Kirshner, Don, 16, 18
Klemmer, John, 218
Klingman, Mark, 222
Knepper, Jimmy, 214
Koerner, Spider John, 79
Konikoff, Sandy, 148, 149, 150
Ko-op Productions, 38
Kooper, Joan, 138, 141, 149, 169
Kooperfone, 114-16
Kooper Session introducing Shuggie Otis, 223
Krackow, Eric, 114, 115
Kristofferson, Kris, 142, 234
Kulberg, Andy, 79, 83, 84, 106, 107, 112-14

Ladies of the Canyon, 242
Langhorne, Bruce, 78
Laurie Records, 29-30
Lay, Sam, 60, 88
Let It Bleed, 239
Levine, Irwin, 38-42, 46, 51, 70
Lewis, Gary, 45
Lieber, Jerry, 16
"Like a Rolling Stone," 56, 59, 60, 66, 76

Lind, Bob, 88
Lipsius, Fred, 157, 159, 160, 164, 165, 167, 174-76, 179
"Little Lonely One," 38
Live Adventures of Mike Bloomfield and Al Kooper, The, 204, 213, 238
"Long Haired Boy," 193
"Looking at a Baby," 193
Los Angeles, California, 102, 137-38
Los Angeles Fantasy Orchestra, 150
Lovin' Spoonful, 79, 88
Lundvall, Bruce, 190
Lynne, Jeff, 175

McCarty, Jim, 129
McCoy, Charlie, 206, 234, 236, 237
McFarland, Gary, 77
"Magic In My Sox," 213
Mamas and the Papas, 144, 185
Mamudes, Victor, 70
Mandala, 125, 129
Manhattan Transfer, 231
Mann, Barry, 18
Marden, Pauline, 150
Markowitz, Roy, 231
Marshall, Jim, 186
Martin, George, 185
Marx, Emmaretta, 120
Mason, Dave, 216
Masse, Laurel, 231
Mayfield, Curtis, 166, 186
Merkin, Trixie, 196
Messina, Jim, 182
MGM-Verve, 90, 100
Midler, Bette, 222
Mihok, Mike, 17
Miles, Buddy, 129, 148
Miller, Jimmy, 238, 239
Miller, Steve, 188, 200
Mitchell, Joni, 242, 243
"Modern Adventures of Plato, Diogenes and Freud, The," 164
Modern Jazz Quartet, 218
Monck, Chip, 140, 141, 144, 215
Monterey Pop Festival, 139-44, 146

Montreal Expo, 104-6
Moog, Robert, 114
Moon, Keith, 126, 129
"More & More," 206
Morgan, Bob, 99
Moss, Wayne, 206, 234, 237
Mothers, 173
"Mourning Glory Story," 213
Move, 238
Muldaur, Maria, 83
Murdoch, Bruce, 79
Murray The K, 125
Music From Big Pink, 162
Music of Bulgaria, 146
Musicor Records, 31, 34
"My Days Are Numbered," 149, 158, 162
"My Kind of Love," 29-30
Mystics, 27
"My Sweet Lord," 19

Naftalin, Mark, 90, 227
Nashville, 206, 232-37
Neapolitan, Ray, 218
Nelson, Ricky, 21, 34
Neuwirth, Bob, 61-64, 68, 150, 216
Nevins, Al, 18
Newman, Randy, 34-35, 165
Newport Folk Festival, 59-60, 118
New York City, 15-19
"New York City (You're a Woman)," 15
New York Jews for Electric Blues crusade, 83
Nilsson, Harry, 165, 213
Nitszche, Jack, 102
"No Time Like the Right Time," 132
Nyro, Laura, 193

Ochs, Alice, 124, 166
Ochs, Phil, 62, 78, 79, 124, 243
Odetta, 156
"Oh Happy Day," 214
Ondioline, 114-16
Orbison, Roy, 34

Orleans, 222
Ostin, Mo, 158
Otis, Johnny, 221-22
Otis, Shuggie, 222-23
Owens, Frank, 76
Ozark Mountain Daredevils, 142

Pappalardi, Felix, 79
Pariser, Alan, 139, 140, 142
Parks, Van Dyke, 139
Passions, 27
Paupers, 194
Paxton, Tom, 243
Pell, Dave, 103
Pell, Stanley, 103
Perry, Jean Jacques, 114
Perry, Richard, 18
Peter, Paul and Mary, 60, 79
Pet Sounds, 146
Phillips, John, 142
Phone Booth, 118, 120
Pickett, Wilson, 125, 129, 148
Pitney, Gene, 32-34, 46, 115, 165
"Plunkin," 31
Pointer Sisters, 183
Pollard, Michael J., 68
Polley, Stanley, 212-13
Powell, Seldon, 215
Powers, Tony, 158
Presley, Elvis, 16, 233
Pridden, Bob, 129
Projections, 116
Prokop, Skip, 194, 198
"Proud Mary," 214
Purdie, Bernard, 214

Queen Booking Corporation, The, 18
"Queen Jane Approximately," 59

Ragavoy, Jerry, 186
Rainey, Chuck, 214
Rand, Ray, 18, 37, 38, 39
Rapp, Charles, 18
Rascals, 118

Redding, Otis, 164, 165
Reed, Jimmy, 16, 78
Reed, Lou, 130
Reynolds, Malvina, 118
Rhinoceros, 148
Rising Sons, 153
Robbins, Hargus, 234, 235-36
Robertson, Robbie, 61, 72, 232, 234
Rockwell, Norman, 202-04
Rogers, Leo, 18, 21-24, 26, 27
Rolling Stones, 238-40
Ronstadt, Linda, 186
Rose, Tim, 183, 193, 194
Ross-Myring, Brian, 221
Rothchild, Paul, 62, 78
Royal, Ernie, 214
Royal Teens, 18, 23, 24, 27
Rubinson, David, 183, 185, 193
Rundgren, Todd, 222
Rush, Tom, 77, 78
Ryder, Mitch, 125, 129

Sacred Cow, 70
San Francisco, California, 124
San Francisco State College Folk Festival, 118
Santana, Carlos, 200, 201, 206
Schactman, Danny, 21-22
Schlinger, Sol, 214
Schoenbaum, Jerry, 92, 182
Schroeder, Aaron, 18, 30-31, 32-34, 45, 46, 144, 182, 213
Scully, Rock, 196
Sea Lark, 30
Sear, Walter, 213
"Season of the Witch," 188
Sebastian, John, 83
Sedaka, Neil, 18
Seeger, Pete, 243
Shannon, Del, 116
Shapiro, Ben, 139
Shelton, Robert, 94
Shirelles, 38
"Sick Manny's Gym," 31
Silver, Horace, 176
Simon, Carly, 77

Simon, Jerry, 228
Simon, John, 162, 164, 166-67, 184-85
Simon, Lucy, 77
Simon, Paul, 50, 144, 155, 204, 228
Simon and Garfunkel, 149, 150, 162, 228
Sims, Zoot, 214, 215
Sledge, Percy, 165
Slick, Darby and Grace, 124
Sloan, P. F., 68
"Smiling Phases," 206
Smith, Keely, 39
Solomon, Howard, 90, 92, 94, 155, 156, 159, 160, 182
"Somethin' Goin' On," 174, 206
"So Much Love," 165, 168
Sons of Adam, 124
South, Joe, 234, 237
Spann, Otis, 92, 93, 120
Spector, Phil, 34, 102, 185
Spier, Larry, Jr., 40
Spirit, 153
Spoelstra, Mark, 118
Springsteen, Bruce, 34, 183
Stamm, Marvin, 214, 215
Steve Paul's Scene Club, 104, 124, 130
"Steve's Song," 96
Sticky Fingers, 240
Stills, Steve, 188, 190, 194, 197, 243
Stoller, Mike, 16
Stony Brook University, blues festival at, 108-110
"Stranger in a Strange Land," 79
Strazza, Peter, 148
Strozier, Frank, 218
Strzelecki, Henry, 234
"Subterranean Homesick Blues," 53
Super Session, 190, 193, 194, 198, 206, 212, 213
Swarthmore College, 97-98

Taj Mahal, 153, 183, 185
Take a Little Walk with Me, 77-78
"Talking Radio Blues," 53
Taupin, Bernie, 244
Taylor, Derek, 140

254 | Index

"Thirty-eight People," 51-52
"This Diamond Ring," 45
"This Wheel's on Fire," 188
Three Dog Night, 139
Three Suns, 18
Thunder, Johnny, 39
"Times They Are A-Changin', The," 49
Tokens, 19, 88
"Tombstone Blues," 59, 64
Townshend, Peter, 126
"Town Without Pity," 34
Traffic, 204
Troiano, Dom, 129
Tubon, 114-16
"Two Trains Running," 111

United States of America, 183

Van Ronk, Dave, 62, 83, 108
Vee, Bobby, 34, 45, 88
Verve-Folkways, 90, 92, 94, 100, 182
Village Gate, 140
Vincent, Stan, 28
Vinton, Bobby, 88, 99
"Violets of Dawn," 84
"Visions of Johanna," 235, 237

"Wake Me Shake Me," 96
Warner Brothers, 158
Waters, Muddy, 16, 77, 87, 92, 93, 108, 120
Watrons, Billy, 214
Waxman, Lou, 166

Webman, Hal, 38-39, 41-42
Webster, Dick, 70
Webster, Guy, 139-40
"Weight, The," 204
Weill, Cynthia, 18
Weiss, Danny, 148
Weiss, Jerry, 159, 172, 173, 179, 181
Well, Junior, 190
We Three Music, 39
Wexler, Jerry, 158
What's Shakin', 79-80
Who, 125, 126, 144
Wilkes, Tom, 140
William Morris Agency, 96, 104
Williams, Big Joe, 92
Wilson, Brian, 25, 139, 146-47
Wilson, Tom, 47, 53, 54, 55, 56, 79, 80, 90, 92, 111, 130
Winwood, Stevie, 79, 175, 206
"Without Her," 165
Wolf, Howling, 16, 120
Wolf, Peter, 230
Woods, Stu, 222
Wow Grape Jam, 183

Yarrow, Peter, 60
"You Can't Catch Me," 102
"You Don't Love Me," 190
"You Make Me So Very Happy," 206
You Never Know Who Your Friends Are, 213
Young, George, 214

Zappa, Frank, 120, 148
Zeppelin, Led, 61

ML 420 .K8 A3   42,532

Kooper, Al.
　　Backstage passes

ML 420 .K8 A3   42,532

Kooper, Al.
　　Backstage passes

DATE DUE

APR 19 1988			
MAY 25 '93			

Property of
LIBRARY
MITCHELL COMMUNITY COLLEGE
Statesville, N. C.   28677

Mitchell Community College LRC
MCC020383